CHILDREN'S WORDS

Children's Words

A practical guide to helping children
overcome difficulties in learning to read,
write, speak and spell

Donald Moyle

First published in 1982 by
Grant McIntyre Limited
90/91 Great Russell Street
London WC1B 3PY

Copright © Donald Moyle 1982

This title is available in both hardback and paperback
editions. The paperback edition is sold subject to the
condition that is shall not, by way of trade or otherwise,
be lent, resold, hired out or otherwise circulated
in any form of binding or cover than that in which it is
published, and without a similar condition, including
this condition, being imposed on the subsequent purchaser.

All rights reserved. No part of this publication may be
reproduced in any form or by any means, electronic or
mechanical, including photocopy, recording, or any information
storage or retrieval system, without permission in writing
from the publisher.

British Library Cataloguing in Publication Data

Moyle, Donald
  Children's words: a practical guide to
  helping children overcome difficulties in
  learning to read, write, speak and spell.
  1. Children–Language
  I. Title
  401'.9   LB1139.L3

ISBN 0–86126–032–4
ISBN 0–86126–033–4 Pbk

Printed and bound in Great Britain
at The Pitman Press, Bath

Contents

	Acknowledgements	vi
	Preface	1
1	Language learning	3
2	Approaches to language teaching	29
3	Diagnostic teaching	88
4	Language across the curriculum	202
	References	207
	Suggestions for further reading	209
	Index	211

Acknowledgements

The study areas of Language and Reading have produced a wealth of research, theory and professional experience over the past two decades. Consequently any new publication must draw heavily upon the ideas and experiences of others. I must, therefore, make general acknowledgement to all who, by their specialized knowledge or professional adventure have contributed to my own understanding.

Specifically I must express special gratitude to Jean Ainslie, Frank Potter and the experienced teachers who have joined me at Edge Hill College of Higher Education over the years for courses of advanced study. Their labours have produced a number of the examples used here to illustrate the classroom and diagnostic practices.

I should like to thank the following authors and publishers for permission to reproduce the material listed below:

'Fluffy's Aeroplane' (p. 69) from Kate and Fluffy Books (*Language Patterns*, Holt, Rinehart & Winston); 'Jack and Jill' (p. 75) from Story Method Books (*Language Patterns*, Holt, Rinehart & Winston); 'The Big Red Lorry' (p. 77) from *Gay Way Scheme* (Macmillan); 'In the Village' (p. 80) from *One, Two, Three and Away* (Hart-Davis); 'Lucy Maud Montgomery' (p. 81) from *Language Patterns* (Holt, Rinehart & Winston); 'Pat's Hat' (p. 144) from Story Methods Books (*Language Patterns*, Holt, Rinehart & Winston); 'Wilbur's New Home'

(p. 164) from *Language Patterns* (Holt, Rinehart & Winston); 'The Fight for Freedom' (p. 170) from *Teaching Reading Seminar* (Holmes McDougall); 'Smugglers' (p. 179), 'Irrigation' (p. 183) and 'Sky Diving' (p. 185) from *Reading Routes* by John Leedham (Longman); 'Who Likes Animals?' (p. 191) from *Rading Development Courses Text* (Open University).

Preface

This book is intended as a practical guide for teachers and parents who want to help their children learn to read, write, speak or spell. Originally I had been asked to write a book of guidance on how to teach children experiencing language difficulties. But thinking over what such a book should cover, I became convinced increasingly that, with the possible exception of children with very severe disabilities, the most appropriate teaching approaches and materials were those which were most apt for the child making normal educational progress. Any book, therefore, which applied to the treatment of difficulties should equally relate to their prevention. Increasingly the view has been gaining ground that the roots of educational, personal and social failure are to be located in language problems, and yet it is only in recent years that serious attempts have been made to study language and so gain insights into how it is learned and might most successfully be taught. Even where this has been undertaken, such work has largely taken the form of erecting general principles rather than giving practical advice, or has been related to only one element of the language arts.

This book therefore begins by discussing our current understanding of how language is learned and the principles whereby ways of teaching and learning are selected, materials chosen and areas of difficulty identified. Chapter 2 describes and gives examples of an integrated approach to developing the language arts both at home and at school, while chapter 3 proposes ideas for, and examples of situations where children's language needs may be informally diagnosed. Throughout the book examples of frameworks are also proposed for more scientific analysis of the informal observations and various suggestions are outlined for follow-up activities.

1

Language learning

The changing faces of language and language learning

Periodically angry voices are raised at the decline of standards. This is nothing new; such charges have been heard ever since education began, that standards are not what they were in the past, and that the way to restore lost excellence is to return to traditional organization and teaching methods.

My aim here is not to discuss the validity of tests, the thorny difficulties of equating the results of one survey with another, or whether recent surveys do demonstrate significant rises or falls in standards. Rather, the question of standards is referred to because it is widely held at present that an education system's progress can be assessed by comparing the current attainment of children with that of children of similar age some years earlier in identical areas of learning. Yet such a view takes no account of those wider changes in society which may have taken place, demanding new objectives and therefore a different educational curriculum.

The rate of change and expansion of knowledge, the re-orientation of the social order, the wider demands made upon the individual by democratic societies and technological progress, these are just a few of the many influences which necessitate very different curricula for our schools today. Whether or not standards in certain areas are higher or lower than in the past is irrelevant to any judgement of the success of a particular educational system. Equally, methods which produced good results in the past may not be applicable to today's children or to the objectives of current curricula. We must therefore consider first of all those changes in society and contemporary culture which affect language and language learning so that we may draw up new objectives for our curricula, and select appropriate materials and teaching strategies.

Changes in society and its needs

The twentieth century has witnessed an incredible acceleration in human and social developments. So much so that very few elements of people's life-styles remain unaffected. Such extensive change demands a different type of educational provision; it would indeed be ridiculous to suggest that the type of elementary education available in 1900, successful as that may have been in its day, could provide a realistic preparation for children for their responsibilities as tomorrow's adults. But what are the changes which specifically affect language and learning?

The process of democratization

Not too many years ago, the lives of most individuals were largely governed by rules, instructions and beliefs set by a small number of individuals and agreed by such bodies as governments or the church. The consensus of opinion supported these authoritarian structures and people were expected to follow the instructions given.

More recently the validity of most institutions has been acutely questioned and each individual has to set his or her own rules for personal living and learn to cooperate in the making of policies, whether at governmental level or on the shop floor, office or in the home. If these more democratic procedures are to have any success each adult must make a contribution. And for that contribution to be worth while the individual must develop a wider knowledge base, and be capable both of considering information and ideas at a deeper level and making judgements.

All the available evidence suggests that the present rate of change will continue; much currently accepted knowledge, and many institutions and standards, are likely to be superseded within the lifetime of today's child. We cannot, therefore, stick to the educational aims of the past which by and large saw the schools as programming instruction to slot their children into a certain place in a certain society. Instead today's children must be prepared for a context which we cannot fully envisage, but which will demand that each individual is capable of accepting and adapting to new systems and understandings. Education, therefore, should aim to prepare the child for the future, and not only the present; to produce versatile and independent thinkers and not conformists. Such an objective makes considerable demands upon language and thinking, particularly when much of such thought will be abstract rather than concrete.

Changes in children

Not surprisingly changes in the adult world have brought about changes among the children in our schools. No longer are children required to be so unquestioningly obedient to adult opinion; they expect and are expected to see the value and usefulness of anything they are asked to do; and they want to know why given procedures need to be followed. They are perhaps more materialistic than in the past, demanding immediate advantages, and will not be put off by suggestions that some learning they undertake now will be beneficial in the future. Similarly, the Protestant ethic of hard work and deferred gratification being good for the soul is unlikely to be acceptable to them: if they are to give of their energies fully in school, the learning experiences must be pleasurable. All this adds up to the realization that the contemporary school must treat children as full partners in learning rather than as vessels to be filled.

One further significant change is that children, on average, first enter school with wider knowledge and a more extensive command of language than in the past. But two particular factors need to be noted if we are to take full advantage of this. Firstly, since society encourages the individuality of language we must beware of attempting to eradicate dialect in preference for a standard English form, and at the same time we must ensure that any mismatch of language forms between teacher and child and text and child is not allowed to form a barrier to learning. Secondly, for all their greater fluency and broader knowledge many children have not had the guidance from adults which they need to help them establish and refine concepts. Recently a teacher suggested that watching a great deal of television had the same effect as rote learning – the children had the knowledge but to use it the child had first to be cued into the particular programme where he or she had heard and seen it. For learning to be of real value it must be possible to relate it to other items so that it may be called upon whenever it is needed. It is perfectly possible for teacher and child to feel they have understood each other but, owing to the great differences in their concepts of the meanings of the words used, no communication has really taken place. For example, five-year-olds will use 'word' in their speech, but if asked to distinguish a word from a letter or even a picture some may be unable to do so.

The knowledge explosion

When the Bullock Committee (1975) reported it suggested that whatever view was taken of language and literacy standards achieved in schools, there was no doubt that they should be higher and more appropriate to the needs of adults. Why higher? Three factors seem to be at work. Firstly, in the early part of this century the type and organ-

Language learning

ization of adult working life meant that in the region of 80 per cent of adults could discharge their work making little use of language or literacy. Today less than 10 per cent of the population escape a dependence on literacy as an integral part of their daily work. It is the same in private life: the need to complete forms, for example, has increased tenfold in the past forty years. Secondly, the necessity of being better informed and involved in society's decision making again demands a wider involvement of language to communicate information and ideas. Without this, ignorance and prejudice can distort and disrupt social life. But thirdly and most influential has been the vast and ever-growing increasing in and diversity of the accumulated learning of the human race. In order to make use of this and contribute to it the individual adult must develop a much wider vocabulary and a matching sensitivity to the variation of meanings that can be indicated by words and to the handling of far more complex sentence structures.

This can be clearly illustrated by a few examples from recent research. It was long held that the *Daily Mirror* was the simplest newspaper from the point of view of its level of reading difficulty. The suggestion was that it could be read by an adult whose reading ability was only that of a nine-year-old child. Some years ago this was certainly true, but by the early 1970s the average reading difficulty presented by the *Daily Mirror*, despite the fact that it was still Britain's easiest to read daily, had risen to an age level of twelve-and-a-half. In the same way the reading demands of official literature and forms, despite efforts to simplify them, have risen greatly and even the safety instructions on domestic commodities usually have a reading demand above the average reading level of sixteen-year-olds. Even in schools the reading difficulty level of textbooks presented to twelve-year-olds is equivalent to the reading level of average fourteen-year-olds.

Clearly, to meet the demands of current levels of reading required by adults in our society new targets are necessary.

It has been suggested that our children of seven-and-a-half years should be able to read as well as the average child of nine years at the moment, and the eleven-and-a-half-year old equate with the level currently achieved by the fourteen-year-old. Nor is this the only challenge. For equally we must greatly extend the range of language and literacy tasks which our children can complete successfully and yet ensure that their attitudes to reading as an activity lead them to desire to read for pleasure.

Why did the Bullock Committee also say that schools' literacy standards should be more appropriate to the needs of adults? There is a growing body of evidence to suggest that language learning in schools is far too narrow to prepare the child for the diversity of demands that will be met in adult life. Many researchers (see Lunzer & Gardner 1979; Murphy, 1973) have suggested that children and adults who in the general sense have quite good levels of language and reading development fail miserably on many everyday tasks. Many adults, for example, fail in following such simple instructions as 'Take two tablets three times a day after meals' where total accuracy is essential.

Indeed it would appear that adults have only a limited range of strategies when it comes to using language. They perform reasonably when the task parallels one in which they are well practised but poorly when there is a need to act in a slightly different manner or to build a new strategy; even though they may have all the knowledge and skills necessary to carry out the new strategy, they cannot align them appropriately. This problem of transferring learning suggests that children should experience a wider range of language situations than at present and become much more conscious of how and why they use language.

Changes in our understanding of language

For many years the study of language was largely confined

to describing its nature and composition. But more recently much greater attention has been paid to the purposes it serves and to the individual person as an active processor of language and information. The weighting of studies towards the understanding and classification of sound and writing systems led to the teaching of language as a set of pronunciation, spelling and syntactical rules. Once language is recognized as an active process, then teaching must turn to explaining how language works to frame, consider and express meaning.

Recent studies have suggested that there are parallels between experience, and thinking and language development, each contributing to the total picture and aiding the development of the others. From an educational point of view, the aspect most deserving attention is the function of language: what is language used for? From the earliest stages of language development the child's speech is motivated by personal needs – to gain satisfaction, to regulate the behaviour of others, to describe the environment, to establish personal relationships. It would seem that at first the prime function of language is to express meaning, and that vocabulary, grammar and intonation are developed subsequently to achieve more effective satisfaction of the individual's requirements.

Translated into educational terms, it appears that the encouragement of language development is best based on the individual child's need to receive and impart meanings. At the same time we must ensure that the full range of language functions are encouraged by the way the environment is structured. For example, it is very easy in school to emphasize, say, the imparting of information and ignore the imaginative or personal relationship functions. Such restrictions must interfere with the development of thinking and the communication aspects of language. For example, do we devote excessive practice to listening to language and insufficient experience to speaking?

Changes in our understanding of reading

Descriptions of the reading process as carried out by the adult efficient reader have long been a part of basic language studies. But although such models have frequently influenced teaching, many other considerations need to be taken into account, and assumptions made before a model for teaching can reasonably be devised. There are, for example, the differences between adult and child in terms of knowledge and the sophistication of their thinking strategies, the manner in which learning is most successfully accomplished, the social environment from which the children come, and even the physical constraints of each school's environment.

Reading letters and words

One model of reading which still has considerable influence upon the teaching of reading, and even more upon remedial teaching, has been around for many decades. According to this the reading act began with the viewing of letters which were then combined into words and later the words were combined to comprehend the author's meaning. Reading seemed, therefore, a passive activity where the recognition of words was paramount and the emphasis was upon the perceptual processes. Re-expressed as a model for teaching, it suggested that the learner should approach the simplest and most regular elements first and over the years gradually master elements of increasing complexity and irregularity. Consequently reading in the classroom began with exercises for discriminating between letters and relating them to sounds, then moved to using these elements in the recognition of words and finally arrived at examining meaningful strings of words. The task for the beginner was thus very different from that of an adult who reads for meaning first and employs the more mechanical aspects of perception and word recognition as secondary support skills.

This model, however, poses other, equally serious problems. Memorizing spoken and written words for a start, is far more difficult in isolation from a meaningful language context. One has only to compare the time it takes to memorize a list of nonsense syllables compared with a list of words whose meaning is known already.

Likewise an approach which divides the teaching of a complex task like reading into its component parts raises the practical difficulty of how to reassemble all the parts. It is not uncommon to find a child who can undertake a task which is part of the total process, such as breaking down a word into its component letters and sounds and then blending these elements together to produce a word (this process refers to the teaching of phonics), but cannot apply the same skill to unknown words encountered when reading a story. Learning in isolation has resulted in the child having a skill that cannot be transferred to other situations because there is no awareness of how, when and where to apply it.

Jerome Bruner (1974) points out that this difficulty in transferring learning is made even harder because the learning task is changed when one element is learned in isolation. For instance, in the preceding example of phonics, children are put in a position where they can only use their knowledge of sound association with symbols; but in context such knowledge works hand in hand with the elements of meaning and grammar, providing a wider, interactive support for the identification of a word.

Learning the sounds

A number of learning programmes attempt to teach the appreciation of what is seen (visual perception) or the ability to separate and recognize sounds (auditory perception) in isolation. Such exercises are still employed widely, especially in remedial education, despite the considerable body of research evidence which suggests that they have little effect upon the growth of reading ability. Again, this may be the result of too narrow an isolation of skill learning. If one looks at the use of auditory and visual perception, the beginning reader is being asked to associate symbols or words on a page with sounds within his spoken language vocabulary store. Simply seeing the written language is insufficient for any meaningful recognition. What is necessary is to be able to relate and place in appropriate sequence a spatial layout in written language with a time order in spoken language, which demands careful thought. And no matter how much practice is given in these isolated skills they will only benefit reading when they are learned together.

Reading and linguistics

One feature of reading largely ignored by the older psychological models is its base in language. The assumption was that in learning to read the child had already mastered spoken language and simply had to match the spoken language to the new written form. Linguists then began to draw attention to the fact that there were many new elements of language to be learned, owing to such things as the vagaries of the spelling, the sound to symbol relationships, and the grammatical styles often present in written language which are not normally used in spoken language. As a consequence one group of linguists devised reading programmes where spelling was the basic element to be mastered on the grounds that the first task in learning to read was to gain automatic recognition of all the major spelling patterns. Learning was ordered in terms of hierarchies of words: from simple to complex, and from regular to irregular. Again, the emphasis being on mere word learning at the expense of meaning, the children spent long periods on mechanical practice before they could enjoy a story. Equally inhibiting was the fact that since the proponents of this approach felt that writing was unnecessary in the early stages, the aid to learning of a multi-sensory input was not available (i.e. the contribution of writing with its aid to memorization through the senses of touch and movement and demonstration of the importance of sequencing of letters).

According to a second group of linguists much greater importance should be attached to the grammar and meaning of language. They insisted that written language had to be learned in meaningful units, at least in the first instance, the smallest such unit being the sentence. Such an approach is obviously connected with the sentence method approach to teaching reading which had been proposed earlier but which had never gained any widespread popularity since no learning activities were incorporated to help the child also learn the role of letters and words within the sentence.

Reading and the reader

This emphasis on meaning and the more detailed understanding of how the individual processes language led to the popularity in recent years of the *psycholinguistic* view. Unlike most earlier models which had treated the reader as a rather passive participant who simply received meaning from a text, psycholinguistic models emphasize the active role of the reader. The suggestion is that the reader sets out by marshalling the relevant background knowledge of subject matter, of vocabulary and grammar relating to his text, checks what he is to read against this background, and then reads with an expectancy of the meaning of the content before him and the satisfaction of personal needs.

Clearly a distinctly new element has been introduced and attention switched from looking at reading merely from the point of view of the nature of written language to considering the needs and mental processes of the actual reader. In the last few years research has concentrated on the interaction between the content of style and meaning and the mental processes of the reader. All of which suggests that the teaching of reading should begin with meaning and that only when children are involved in processing meaning will they be able to master the more mechanical aspects of word recognition.

Instead of the older view that mastery of words came first and when that had been achieved the child could use this knowledge to unlock the meaning in flows of language, the new view suggests that the ability to recognize words in isolation from a context is a skill which develops at a later stage.

Writers on reading acquisition have tended in recent years, often unwittingly, to hinder the development of teaching approaches which give prime place to the processing of meaning. Much has been written about primary skills (such as word recognition), intermediate skills (the processing of language forms) and higher order skills (the deeper levels of thinking needed for the thorough processing of meaning in text). Consequently some have assumed that there are, in fact, three chronological stages of development in learning. Instead they are simply convenient classifications of the various aspects of the nature of the task and all three should be used together from the earliest stages of learning to read. Aspects of them are already at work in the thinking and spoken language of the child. For example, the two-year-old on hearing a story can usually suggest whether it was a true story or a fairy tale; the type of thinking involved in such a decision would normally be classified as a higher order process. It is possible, therefore, to develop many of the thinking abilities involved in reading in spoken language situations before written language is even introduced.

Though the psycholinguists drew attention to the need to examine reading in terms of meaning for both reader and text, they tended at first to consider that all reading was of one type. Equally they assumed in the case of the learner that, provided an interaction of meanings was taking place, the child's reading skill could be fully developed. But it has already been argued (see p.8) that the nature of the reading task varies according to the purposes of the reader and the type of written language material. For example, the adult reader does not read in the same manner when relaxing with a novel as when studying a textbook for an examination. Obviously a timetable would present a very different reading task if it was being scanned to find the time of the next train than if it was being studied intensively in an effort to organize the efficiency of the total service. In the same way, the reading operation involved in following a recipe to produce a meal demands total accuracy whereas scanning a cookery book to select dishes for a meal requires only reading for general impression. Clearly reading must be considered in terms of the total range of situations and materials in which it is to be practised and the learner is most likely to be successful if the learning is undertaken in skill-using situations across the whole school curriculum.

Equally, one could deduce from some psycholinguists that, providing the material a child uses has meaning, the problems of learning will be overcome. This ignores the fact that any reading will only be meaningful to a child who desires to know the meaning present in the text. This touches on two important points.

If the only premise was that a text had to have meaning in itself before a child could learn, then almost any text at an appropriate level of difficulty could be used. On the other hand, if the decisive factor is that the text is meaningful to the child, then it is essential to choose texts which provide the information and enjoyment the child needs and desires.

But such careful choice of texts is important not only because it makes learning easier but because of the far-reaching effects it has on attitudes. Malformed attitudes to reading are increasingly seen as a major cause of reading failure. The formation of good attitudes not only stems from whether parents and other persons important to the child are seen to use and value reading, but is significantly affected by the extent to which the child understands the nature of the task and sees it as being personally useful and enjoyable.

Changes in our understanding of word 'identification'

Listening and reading have interesting parallels in terms of the identification of individual words. If a word is spoken in isolation without prior warning it is often difficult to identify, but when the same word occurs in the context of a conversation it appears to be recognized with little conscious effort. The explanation, of course, is that through the context the mind is being prepared for the individual word by the meaning provided by other words but also for the likelihood of certain words occurring in particular sequences from the reader's background knowledge of grammar. Without the cues of context, the listener has only the sounds of the individual word to help him and no other guides to overcome any misgivings or confusions.

Children have developed a good deal of expertise in the use of context by the time they are five years old. Equally, they can very often make good responses on the basis of grammatical form alone. Consequently even when they are not accurate in terms of meaning, if asked to supply a missing word in a sentence, they can supply, orally, a word that fits the bill. For example, in the sentence 'The girl runs – the road', the child may insert words such as *along*, *up*, or *down*, but it is most unlikely that a verb or noun will be suggested. The child seems to know intuitively which part of speech is appropriate even though he or she would not be able to explain what parts of speech such as adverbs or nouns are.

If this is true, it seems illogical to ignore the spoken language attainment of children by asking them to master word learning in the early stages of reading only by memorizing whole words and/or phonic analysis. It would be far more apt to supplement the basic approach with the use of context and establish the following code for the child's attack on an unknown word in reading:

1 What do you think the author means?
2 Does the sort of word seem to fit?
3 Does the word you thought of look and sound like the one the author used?

One should proceed with a certain amount of caution, however, for work on isolated words can often lead to the ability to recognize such words but not really identify them. The distinction is between being able to make an appropriate sound in response to the printed word but not being aware of its meaning or grammatical function in the text.

Research suggests that it is much harder to learn words in isolation than to learn them in context, for though the mind can only consider a few letters at a time it can simultaneously appreciate a few words or indeed a sentence or more in terms of ideas. It would seem wiser, therefore, to encourage the child to pay attention to the largest unit rather than expend mental energy in a less rewarding manner by giving overdetailed attention to letters. It can indeed be argued that the automatic identification of words presented in isolation is one of the later elements of the reading process to appear and not the first step in learning to read.

Language difficulty

Language difficulties can arise from a wide range of very different situations. Problems of hearing, permanent or temporary, which restrict the amount and/or clarity of the language received from others, result in a lack of language stimulation. Speech defects limit the ability of the child to produce language freely and thus hinder the practice necessary for consolidating the learning. Other children are limited by the lack of language stimulation in their environment, which retards language and general development. Most significant here of course, as a problem in schools are those for whom English is a second language. They may have inadequate speech models at home or may even only hear English spoken in school. Obviously for them the encouragement of language acquisition may need to parallel the typical stages passed through by the pre-school child. This is complicated, however, by the fact that their intellectual development may have moved ahead at a reasonable rate in relation to the development of their first language, and therefore the work they are asked to undertake may seem uninteresting.

With all forms of low language development the basic problem is that any retardation of language affects all other activities, attainments and abilities. Since language is a necessary base skill in the interpretation and extension of the individual's experience of the world, any linguistic retardation is liable to become generalized and likely to affect the emotions, attitudes and aspirations. For example children who have below-average levels of language development also usually suffer from below-average abilities in visual perception. Originally such children clearly enjoyed the normal range of visual experiences, but a lack of language stimulation appears to have prevented their developing labels, explanations and schemas of meaning to understand the experiences fully, integrate them into their memories and recall the information when it is useful in new situations.

Such a combination of disability in both language and perception poses obvious problems for learning to read and write. In the reading situation the stimulus upon the page must be processed visually and related to the existing spoken language knowledge before any response can be made. Equally, in writing the child must frame a message through spoken language and then transpose it into written form. Here the visual task is even more complicated as the forming of letters and spelling of words demands a greater degree of exactness and the memorization of shape and sequence than does reading.

But there is an even more basic source of difficulties. Frequently it is not until children enter school that they find challenges that must be met and not simply coped with or avoided. Whereas preschool life has been reasonably satisfying, they begin to feel that school is not a happy place and may well form attitudes towards learning and school that view it at best as an unavoidable evil and at worst as a punishment from which they must escape at the earliest possible moment.

Of course society, inadequate language stimulation in the home, lack of medical attention or the poverty of provision of nursery school education in Britain are all blamed. But that does not help in solving the problem for the child. Though other agencies may be able to help in various ways, the major positive influence will be the extent to which parents and teachers can stimulate language development.

How this stimulation of language development may be achieved will be examined in some detail later in this book. Here we will simply look at the principles which could guide practice, taking as our starting point the current debate arising from sociological theories of language disabilities.

Two accounts of language disability

The two extreme views in this debate have been termed the *difference* and *deficit* hypotheses. The *difference* hypothesis states that all the language necessary for learning is present but that through the influence of such things as dialect the language employed by the child has a mismatch with that normally acceptable in school and wider society. The 'deficit' hypothesis suggests that the language currently used by the child is insufficient to allow for effective learning and development.

The former hypothesis arose from a study of linguistic

differences between white and black Americans whilst the latter was related to the apparently superior educational performance of middle-class as opposed to working-class groups. It is not important here to delve into the details or validity of these theories but it is interesting to examine whether either one leads to the possibility of providing a framework for effective learning.

If we accept the difference hypothesis then the instruction the child should receive basically should be within the confines of his social or dialect group language. In the extreme all books would be published to conform to the language types evinced by the major subgroups in our society. Apart from the economic and organizational difficulties, such a move would run the risk of great dangers for society since it would increase the distance between groups, making them find it more and more difficult to communicate with each other, share in each other's development and work towards equality of opportunity. There is, however, one major message in the theory that cannot be ignored, namely that for effective learning we must start with the language possessed by the child. Otherwise the new learning will pose more problems for the child as he will be unable to weld it into his past experience and language development. Further, he may feel that not only his language but his family and society are being dismissed as of little value and consequently become resistant to further learning activities to protect his own self-esteem.

By starting from the premise that the language the child possesses is inadequate for effective learning, the deficit hypothesis appears at first sight to be the more destructive of the two theories. It was certainly taken by some as separating the particular social groups into superior and inferior. If, however, we can rid ourselves of the notion that what was being proposed was that everyone must master middle-class, standard English and use received pronunciation then the theory does appear to have a constructive message, which is that the wider the language knowledge the greater will be the opportunities to communicate with and learn from others.

Thus together the two theories give us a workable principle concerning what has to be learned and the point of departure for learning: as wide a range of language as possible and the point of commencement to be the actual language of the individual child. The theories do not, however, give us much help in terms of the teaching approach which should be applied other than the suggestion that in the very early stages some type of language-experience approach will be necessary.

Two views of teaching language disability

Two schools of thought have in recent years been influencing practice in this field. The first, often referred to as *enrichment*, suggests that as language is normally learned in relation to experiences, meaning and personal needs, the child with language disability must be given a wide range of real life experiences with people alongside to help develop language and thinking in relation to them. This would seem quite logical but the approach raises real problems. Which experiences should be selected? Will parent and teacher resources be available to closely supervise the experiences? And most of all, since such an approach is likely to be very lengthy, surely the children are in danger of falling further behind rather than coming closer to the attainment of their more fortunate peers?

The second school of thought has its roots in the more pragmatic approach of behaviourist psychology. It suggests that we should analyse language and then produce programmes through which the child will develop vocabulary and grammar. Ostensibly this must be more economic than the enrichment approach. However, this may not be so since in practice the child may be spending time supposedly learning things he already knows, the work may be ordered in a way which is unsuitable to his learning needs and style or be unrelated to things which he finds realistic and meaningful.

So the one is too haphazard, the other too narrow and structured. Let us, however, draw the good points from each of the approaches from the two areas which we have examined and summarize the consequent principles:

- endeavour to identify the child's individual language attainments and needs.

- start from the stage of development reached and make use of the child's existing language type and knowledge.

- structure the programme for each individual according to his needs and abilities.

- make learning as meaningful and realistic as possible in terms of economy of time by selecting experiences valid for their own sake as well as providing opportunities for language learning.

In fact, these principles will be seen to play a key part in the formulation of the general teaching methods discussed in chapter 2 and the diagnostic teaching examples in chapter 3.

Remedial education

Remedial education has suffered from a plethora of terminology which has often confused many of the issues in the field and led to organizational systems and teaching methods which have not always been appropriate to the needs of children. Historically a child was deemed suitable to profit from such education if his attainment fell below the potential which appeared to be predicted by his ability. *Retarded* was the label often applied to such children and the supposed gap was expressed by comparing the child's mental age with his attainment age in any subject (usually only in reading and mathematics).

Retarded children were often seen as being drawn only from those whose scores on an intelligence test fell within the average or above average range of scores for children of the same age. Those who showed below average scores on ability tests were labelled *backward*, the suggestion being that by virtue of their low ability they would always be slow to learn and their ultimate achievements would likewise always be below average. It is possible, however, that the *backward* child may also be *retarded*, i.e. not working even up to the level of his low ability.

In recent years the field has been further confused by the introduction of an alternative nomenclature intended to eradicate the stigma of the older labels or to describe more precisely the nature of the problem. Examples of the former are 'slow learning', 'learning difficulties' and 'learning disabilities' which say little other than that a child is thought to have some difficulty or difficulties which require some attention. The one major advance here is that a direct link is no longer presumed between the results of ability and attainment tests. Studies have shown repeatedly over the years that the instruments available to assess potential ability have a low level of accuracy. It is far more reliable to study the current behaviour of a child in order to discover learning needs to guide teaching than to trust to targets set by an intelligence test result. The labels, at any rate, continue to be of little value in establishing any direct link between the type of problem and its appropriate treatment.

The more specific labels were coined to try to overcome this lack of a direct link and examples of these are 'autism', lack of ability to communicate; 'dyslexia', severe reading disability related to some neurological malfunction and social disadvantage, lack of a stimulating educational and linguistic background. Although at first sight this alteration may seem to be helpful, unfortunately the link forged is more between cause and problem rather than between need and treatment. Consequently the classifications do not always appear helpful in providing the basis for educational action. Too preoccupied with efforts to label and type children we must direct energies to a more appropriate line of action which will assess their needs as individuals and direct towards the planning of learning and teaching situations.

But there are significant stumbling blocks. To start with the attitudes of society are in need of change, for society has very narrow views as to what is recognized as important and worthwhile. Predictably society tends to view learning from the points of view of its own social, economic and political purposes rather than the needs of the individual. Consequently it sees an immediate return in ensuring that all children become literate but has not much enthusiasm for ensuring that all should have a basic background in geography. It is not surprising, therefore, that most local education authorities have well-developed services to aid children who make little progress in learning to read, many have some investment in helping children with mathematics but there is little or no investment in such areas as music or craft and design.

Two points arise from this. Firstly, society has made its selection of which areas are felt to be important and secondly, it refuses to recognize that children can have learning difficulties in any area. Indeed, it is not uncommon that ability in music or art is considered an innate gift whilst it is assumed all can read. It is self-evident, however, that everyone has areas in which they could have greatly increased attainment. The idea of attainment/ability comparisons and the attitudes of society combine to ignore the fact that many children who are making apparently normal progress for children of their age could, with judicious help, achieve a much higher level of attainment and secondly, that the basic skills of literacy and numeracy are isolated for special attention.

This isolation of the basic skills is one of the major causes of the inadequacy of remedial education; it separates the learning of the skills from the situations where they would normally be used and which provide a realistic environment

Language learning

for their development. The removal of children from their normal classwork to have extra help with the basic skills frequently leads to teaching in relation to the old psychological model of reading where work is on isolated subskills and unrelated to the gaining of information or the enjoyment of a story line. If a child is having difficulty with the total process, he will often experience more difficulty with activities which isolate parts of the activity from the context as a whole. So, far from making the learning easier we may have made it more difficult. Already upset by his lack of progress, the child becomes frustrated by what for him are meaningless activities and since he cannot see the function or purpose of such subskill learning, he is likely to develop limiting attitudes towards learning.

Remedial education, and particularly diagnosis of learning difficulties, has been heavily influenced by the medical model. This model is enshrined legally in the 1944 Education Act where, though the thinking behind the act was laudable in terms of an endeavour to provide education appropriate to the needs of the individual, the suggestion was that children could be correctly placed in special schools according to learning handicaps assessed by a single battery of tests. The same atmosphere permeated through most other aspects of education.

The medical model is one of diagnosis and treatment. The patient is regarded as ill and the symptoms of the illness are tested and classified so that appropriate treatment may be prescribed to effect a cure. Thus if there was a lack of vitamin C, medicine was provided to restore the balance, or if a germ had entered the system it had to be killed off by taking some tablet or other.

Yet even in the medical field today the practitioner attempts to review symptoms in terms of what good health embodies for the individual patient and not in terms of one universal model of human fitness. Too often in education we have been guilty of comparing children with some mythical norm or average child and assessing their supposed problems on the basis of distance from the norm rather than detailed observation of their individual makeup. It seemed hardly unnatural therefore that teachers and psychologists should devote a good deal of time looking for symptoms of difficulty and pin-pointing precise problems in the subskills of learning operations which the non-average child appeared to have. Once diagnosed intensive practice was given in the areas of weakness and apparently faulty behaviour was suppressed.

There are many problems in this approach.

- The presentation of a battery of tests upon which future learning experiences are to be based puts the child under great stress. If one can imagine the child, already feeling depressed by his lack of progress, being put into a nerve-racking test situation where all his weaknesses are being brought clearly before his eyes. No matter how carefully the tester seeks to establish empathy with the child and put him at ease the child is likely to become confused and insecure. Consequently he may not perform in a manner and at a level which is normal for him.

- Testing on materials which are designed to test subskills may result in revealing symptoms of difficulty where real difficulties or problems do not exist. For example, it is common to test phonic ability using lists of nonsense words which conform to precedents in English spelling. However, the normal aid the child can obtain from context to support his phonic abilities has been removed and therefore the task is rather different from the one she may be used to. Also the child may be inhibited because her efforts, though they could present the correct answer, make her feel insecure since the work does not conform to a word she knows. In this situation she may refuse to make a response and so produce a depressed result. Frequently it has been discovered that subskill testing prior to remedial action being taken produces a confusing result for the child's difficulties tend to generalize. She may have no difficulty in her use of visual perception in reading but because of the nature of the test material, her insecurity and confusion in the situation or her attitudes towards the area in general, she produces symptoms which suggest she has a difficulty. Obviously here the provisions of future learning situations designed to overcome a non-existent difficulty are largely a waste of time.

- A contributory element in the situation described above is the fact that there is no clear basis, arising from research, to show that the division of an activity into subskills has any validity. In reading, for example, it may be that individuals can reach the same satisfactory results by very different means. Thus although it is obvious that in all reading tasks visual perception plays a part, for one person it may be a major contributor but for another, by greater dependence upon language, background knowledge and prediction, perception may play only a minor part in the completion of the task.

- Finally, even assuming that the symptoms were accurately assessed and related to real learning difficulties, the needs of the child will quickly change. As soon as some further attainment has been gained there will be new learning needs which may bear no resemblance to the earlier diagnosis. Whereas increased health rarely creates a new medical problem, increased attainment can change the whole pattern of need. Equally, when medical treatment is successful the patient becomes healthy and does not need further treatment. In learning, however, it is important to recognize that at every stage all children, and not only those who have at some time evinced serious learning difficulties, constantly create new needs which must be identified if learning is to progress successfully. It would seem important then that the observation of needs is a constant factor in helping all children and that initial predictions must constantly be revised.

Many past considerations, therefore, require urgent revision to fit current knowledge and experience. What these amount to are summarized as follows and will be used in the search for general teaching approaches in chapter 2 and the more specific diagnostic teaching procedures outlined in chapter 3.

1. Diagnosis must be a continuing feature of language work with all children whether they are falling behind the attainment which is average for their age or not.
2. Diagnosis needs to be undertaken in the context of a total task rather than on materials which purport to assess performance in the subskills supposed to be essential components of the task.
3. Diagnosis should be related to learning operations rather than to the product of the learning.
4. In order to perform normally the child must feel that the task on which she is being observed is realistic and worthwhile for its own sake.
5. Patterns of need should be established to avoid overenthusiastic response to isolated symptoms of difficulty.
6. The child should always be viewed as unique in terms of her abilities, knowledge and the style in which she learns rather than as a comparison with the average child. Equally, any conclusion drawn concerning her needs should be considered in the light of her total personality and not in isolation.
7. Attention needs to be focussed upon the manner in which the child uses language and not upon the inference of needs from narrow observation of the product of her behaviour.

2

Approaches to language teaching

Some criteria for effective language learning

The criteria discussed in what follows are drawn from the previous discussion (see pp.4–28) and the present state of our knowledge of how learning most effectively takes place. It is these criteria which will be used as a basis for the selection of teaching strategies to be employed in the development of language.

Learning and thinking

The relationship between language and thinking in their contribution to learning has long been a strongly contested issue. According to certain authorities language is the basis of all learning, while for others intellectual operations are the decisive factor and language is nothing more than a facilitating instrument. On present evidence, however, language and thinking should be seen as working together so that there is a close match between the stages of language acquisition and other learned elements of child behaviour. Certainly, children who have a lowly level of language development find most types of learning difficult.

For many years it was felt that thinking developed in a series of stages according to a preset order. But recent evidence suggests that quite complicated tasks can be undertaken by young children, if they are set in a context which is appropriate to their level of knowledge and in relation to familiar experiences. Four basic elements, in fact, would seem to be required for the successful achievement of any new learning task: appropriate background knowledge, suitable thinking strategies, a felt need which the individual wishes to satisfy and good attitudes towards the task.

For learning to be meaningful the child must be able to draw upon some previous experience, knowledge or concepts to which the new learning can be related. For example, if the child has not already established a concept of number, then learning a multiplication table will be difficult and hard to assimilate. This would be rote learning of the narrowest kind. It would be equally difficult to learn how to use a map without understanding the points of the compass. For effective and economic learning, therefore, we must put new learning in terms of learning already mastered. It would be a nonsense to ask a child to begin reading unless he already had some mastery of spoken language – though spoken language is but one item in the range of background knowledge and experience which the reading task draws upon.

All learning tasks demand the use of certain thinking processes. In spelling, for example, the child has to master and to commit to memory the visual sequencing of letter order within words. Consequently he will learn to spell much more easily if he has already developed the ability to follow and memorize items set out in a left to right sequence.

Purpose and need

The child who does not feel any need for a certain item of learning is unlikely to apply much energy to the task. An adult, on the other hand, who undertakes any task has normally felt a need to do so and decided to satisfy that need. All too often schools have ignored this factor and children have been expected to undertake learning tasks which have simply been assigned by the teacher. Needs take many forms, however, and must not be confused with mere desire or intrinsic interest. The adult is fully aware of the need to fill in his tax return but the enthusiasm for such a task is unlikely to be high. Nevertheless a purpose is established and it is the purpose which acts as the directing factor. Research increasingly suggests a central place for clear purposes as the basis of the effective completion of a task. If there is no clear purpose for one of the parties to a conversation, for example, the conversation will break down, for attention will not be paid consistently and the messages one member wishes to impart will only be partially received by the other. Again, in reading, unless the reader establishes a clear idea of the type of satisfaction he wishes to gain from a text, he is unlikely to comprehend the text at any depth.

The satisfaction of a need has an obvious effect on the individual's attitude to a task. If there are no clear benefits, motivation to undertake the task will be poor – the individual needs to realize that there are to be outcomes which he finds worth while. If in school a child is continually being subjected to types of learning tasks in which he sees no point, he will develop resistant and negative attitudes. But attitudes are influenced by other major factors, such as the overall response to learning and the value of schooling in general, the success gained in similar tasks in the past and an understanding of the nature of the task. Only too frequently in language learning the child does not understand the task clearly and the instructions sometimes fail to communicate such understanding because of a mismatch between the concepts of the teacher and the level attained by the child. For example, if the child has a poorly defined view of the nature of a word, then instructions given by a teacher asking the child to undertake certain operations, such as 'fill in the missing words' may cause confusion. Observation has shown that even when child and teacher use the same language, the concepts of meaning behind their language are often very different so that the child may use the term 'word' to apply to letters or even sometimes to pictures. Even after a full year at school there are quite a number of children whose concept of a word is still only partially formed. Yet good attitudes towards written language in particular depend upon the child's ability to refine those concepts of language that we employ in talking about language itself.

Purpose, however, is not merely a motivator. It sets all language learning in a real context, thereby making the work meaningful. But much more than this it directs all aspects of a language task, deciding, for example, which language art should be used, whether spoken or written, and if written the particular medium: newspaper, novel, legal document, etc. It is purpose which also selects the thinking strategies to be employed, marshalls appropriate background knowledge, orders the carrying out of the task and prescribes the outcomes. The challenge alike to the teacher in school and the parent at home is to set all tasks intended to encourage language learning in contexts that give the child an outcome of value over and above the immediate language learning. This suggests that language teaching should be taught across the curriculum instead of in separate lessons.

The language arts naturally interact in many of the tasks adults undertake and consequently when learning has a purpose they can be developed in an integrated way. Each channel of communication supports the others. For example, a word which is heard, spoken, read and written is much more likely to be remembered, identified or used in future than one which is met in only one context. Similarly, it is difficult to plan the learning of spoken language if it is undertaken separately from written language, for the latter provides a structure and context on which spoken language activities can be based.

Structure in language learning

This raises the whole question of structure in language

Approaches to language teaching

learning. Too often this has been interpreted only in terms of a present sequence – such as a reading scheme with controlled vocabulary – where the learning of new words is in a given order entirely under the author's control. Yet obviously this can separate the learning from the needs of the child – the learning is superimposed and the child becomes a less active participant. Any text which presents a preset sequence of learning must surely be modified in order to attend to the interests and learning requirements of the child. The result is a new type of structure which emerges from a knowledge of the stage of development and of the abilities of the child and of his current needs in relation to the learning task on which he is currently employed.

Such a structure means that all our language teaching must become diagnostic teaching. The needs, interests, strengths, difficulties and attitudes of the child need to be carefully observed in real situations so that a suitable programme can be planned and modified in the light of continuing observations. How to collect this type of information will be explored in chapter 3.

However, it would be a mistake to assume that all language learning is a matter for interaction at the individual level between child and teacher/parent. For since language is about the communication of meaning the child will naturally wish to communicate with a wider audience. Indeed, the child may often feel restricted in his communication with the teacher, assuming that the teacher already knows all the answers or is simply checking up on him. The child is much more likely to reveal many of his real language needs in a group composed of his peers than in the isolation of individual work which so often appears less immediate.

Controversies concerning teaching approaches

The role of the teacher

Influenced by two particular views of education, teaching methods have tended to concentrate on small areas and types of learning rather than on an overall approach. On the one hand there is the view that the teacher's role is to impart knowledge. This resulted in the development of methods for memorizing subject matter, often revolving around rote learning. According to the other, the teacher's role is basically to encourage the acquisition of those certain skills which would aid learning.

Historically, it came to be assumed that skill learning was the major role of elementary or primary schools whereas secondary schools had the duty of imparting knowledge. No one today would seriously suggest that either role can be entirely separated from the other. Skill learning must always have some content even if that content is used merely as a vehicle for the acquisition of skills. Equally, the mastery of any content involves the learning and development of skills. Nevertheless, our education system still implies that children master skills first and then apply those same skills later to acquire knowledge. All surveys undertaken at primary school level, it will be noted, are of the basic skill attainment type whereas 'O' and 'A' level examinations emphasize achievement in terms of subject matter.

Which is not to issue a challenge to the whole education system. Rather it is to draw attention to the fact that in language learning it has been this second skill-orientated teaching which seems to have had most popularity, with the result that language learning has often been isolated from the content of the curriculum.

Technology and psychology

A considerable boost was given to skill learning procedures

during the 1950s when the need for technological advance and the influence of the Behaviourist school of psychology combined to modify teaching methods and materials. In the field of language learning this influence was perhaps not quite as strong as in other areas of learning since language is somewhat more difficult to present in programmed text than say, mathematics or science. Nevertheless, the general trends of the movement were reflected in the availability of many materials for the development of language and reading.

Unexpectedly the most influential single event was the launching by the Russians of the first Sputnik in 1957 with the immediate criticism that the education systems of the Western world were not producing the skills and knowledge needed to support society's demand for technological understanding and innovation. Comparisons were freely drawn between the movement in the immediate postwar period in the West towards an education primarily directed at the child's current individual needs and that in Russia which, it was suggested, was structured to support the needs of society by ensuring that certain levels and types of skill were developed. One author (Flesch 1955) drew the comparison that whilst American children were learning the nursery rhyme, 'Jack and Jill', Russian children would be working formally upon the calculation of the incline of the hill, the capacity of the pail and the rate of acceleration controlling the speed at which the children fell down the hill.

Programmed learning materials with their carefully graded steps towards the mastery of some skill or knowledge appeared to be the antidote to the problems which many people in society considered were being created by child-centred education. Here was the possibility of precision in learning and a new opportunity to design the curriculum in terms of the needs society had for particular skills and understandings. The arguments raged between protagonists of each of these schools of thought. Even so, history shows that much more careful grading of language learning materials took place during this era; and though few materials for language and reading development were programmed in the full sense of the term, they did reflect the general trend.

'Skill-getting' and 'skill-using'

Many materials were produced in the late 1950s and 1960s and have sold very successfully, under the influence of the psychology of behaviourism. The Reading and Language Laboratories produced by Science Research Associates are quite typical. Significantly, however, these materials have been used much more narrowly than their author, D. H. Parker, intended – no doubt influenced by the contemporary attitudes towards the nature of learning. Parker (1958) set out the intended use of these materials in the following terms. He suggested that education consisted of two processes, the learning of skills which he termed *skill-getting* and the application of skills which he called *skill-using*. When he examined the teaching/learning contexts he felt that *skill-getting* was best achieved by what he described as formal education where the work of the child was highly directed by teacher or materials. Children, he suggested could learn skills from such an approach but the learning may be invalidated because of an inability to apply the learning in tasks which were somewhat different from those on which the skills had been learned. To be freed from this restriction the child must be presented with wide opportunities to apply the skills in a variety of situations. In looking at child-centred informal teaching methods Parker recognized that the problem-solving, discovery, realistic activities gave the opportunity for *skill-using*, but he suggested that they had little to offer in terms of *skill-getting*.

Parker's laboratories were designed as *skill-getting* materials for use over the first third of an academic year. At the same time he asked the teacher to enable these skills to transfer to other situations where they could be used, by spending the other two-thirds of the year in practising those same skills in more realistic *skill-using* situations. Parker claimed that his materials would produce the skill attainment level in three months that normally took a year to achieve and this then left the rest of the year for the child to learn how to make the decisions as to when, where and how to apply them successfully. As noted earlier, however, Jerome Bruner (1974) has challenged the skills model approach. He suggested that one of the major causes of difficulty in transferring learning from a narrow *skill-getting* activity to the realistic complex tasks where it is employed lies in the fact that when skills are isolated from the normal learning context the nature of the skill and its function are changed. Thus it may be that in the second part of Parker's system, the children are not in fact transferring skills but learning the real skills involved for the first time. Even more worrying has been the use to which schools have put Parker's laboratories; by and large they have not been used in a booster manner for only part of the year, and few teachers have endeavoured to arrange situations where the skills practised within the laboratories are applied later in the curriculum.

Noting this problem, John Merritt (1971) devised a simple curriculum model which may also serve as the basis for the organization of a single learning task. The model has divisions: goals, plans, implementation and development (GPID). Merritt's aim was to set the learning of skills and knowledge within one integrated task. In this situation the child is aware of the context and purposes of the learning and therefore learns also the type of task where such behaviour will be of value in the future. Merritt's model may be explained briefly as follows:

Goals   the recognition of personal needs, the setting of purposes and anticipation of outcomes.

Plans	working out how the goals are to be achieved, which content, strategies and skills are to be used. It is at this point that if teacher and child feel some skill or process needs to be learned, instruction can be given and then the skill learned is used immediately in the total task.
Implementation	the carrying out of the procedures to fulfil the goal.
Development	checking on the success in achieving the goals set; deciding what needs to be done with the outcomes gained; considering what new possibilities have arisen which could be further explored.

This model also overcomes another problem in teaching and learning. This is that unless learning is undertaken in relation to the context of a total task then there are a number of skills and operations which may be omitted. Consider for example, a comprehension exercise. In this the child is only involved in word identification and meaning processing. The purpose, the material to be read and the desired results have all been selected by the author. No matter how well the child performs in such a task there is no guarantee that he will be able to apply the learning in realistic tasks which are normally met outside the school.

'Spontaneous' and 'contrived'

At this point it is helpful to consider Joyce Morris's (1975) use of the terms *spontaneous* and *contrived* to describe materials used for the development of reading and the teaching methods associated with them. *Spontaneous* refers to the development of learning through all the experiences of the child, whereas *contrived* refers to teacher and/or author-directed tasks specifically designed to teach particular elements of the total process. Joyce Morris believes that both these approaches should continue in parallel throughout school life.

Spontaneous approaches, of course, have the immediate advantage of placing learning in a more normal setting where skills are learned in the context of their daily use. It is also possible to ensure a better match with the needs and attainments of the individual child than in a setting that has been specially devised. The disadvantages, however, are equally obvious. The teacher has to provide a structure for each individual child's development and therefore must have a considerable understanding of the demands made by each task and a deep knowledge of the needs and abilities of each child. The teacher also has to be available when the child needs support or instruction. In a busy classroom all these demands are probably more than the teacher can reasonably fulfil and inevitably many opportunities to extend the children's learning will be missed despite the meaningful, integrated context.

The *contrived* approach, on the other hand, brings with it the well-recognized transfer of learning problems, omits some of the processes which are part of normal tasks and is more difficult to fit to the needs of the individual child. However, contrived materials and situations have the advantage of providing child and teacher with the security of a readymade structure and lessening the extent to which the teacher needs to prepare materials.

The answer seems to lie in taking the best features of both *contrived* and *spontaneous* approaches and welding them together. Frequently when this has been tried in the past, the attempt has failed because there was no real logic to their integration and the children tended not to relate the various activities to each other. Later in this chapter a framework will be outlined which should help teachers achieve this higher level of integration in their teaching approach.

Children's Words

'Approach' and 'method'

In language work the terms *approach* and *method* are often used interchangeably as synonyms. Personally I find it helpful to use *approach* for the total teaching strategy, learning situations, and materials. *Method*, on the other hand is best restricted to describe individual teaching strategies. Unfortunately it has been common, but unhelpful, to refer to methods under this definition as being capable of the function of the total teaching approach. Thus for many years theorists argued as to the relative merits of whole word and phonic teaching methods as methods of teaching reading. Both, of course, are nothing more than methods of teaching two of the possible strategies a child may use to identify words – the one by memorizing their shape or spelling, the other by equating sounds with the letters of the word and synthesizing the sounds into the form of the word. Bitter arguments developed between protagonists of the two schools of thought and teachers were often asked to teach reading by one method or the other. They were, of course, only teaching aspects of word identification and even if both were used, the third method of word identification, namely the context of grammar and meaning surrounding the individual word was often ignored.

Lists of alternative methods of teaching reading are often included in texts about the teaching of reading and authors tend to evaluate them in terms of their advantages and limitations. In practice it would perhaps be better if they were set out in terms of their contribution to the total development of the child's use of language. For then it would be seen that they all have a place in a total learning approach. But we are all prisoners of past experience and still find it hard to think of language education except in terms of skills and preset orders for development.

Yet our search is for a teaching approach not only for reading but for the whole of language learning, one which is capable of integrating the learning of all the language arts and of being carried out in the meaningful setting of the total curriculum. There are, I believe, two methods of teaching reading which together provide the basis of such an overall approach, namely language-experience and story method, and it is to these that we will now turn.

'Language experience'

Language-experience has long been included in reviews of methods of teaching reading and has featured regularly in the activities employed in classes in infant schools. It was also the basis of the Schools Council research project materials, *Breakthrough to Literacy*. But most of the descriptions of the method are too limited, treating it only as a first introduction to written language and ignoring its value at later stages. As restricting have been the overly narrow definitions of the term *language-experience* so that many have not realized its application to two particular groups of teaching methods.

In its most frequently used form, *language-experience* is defined as presenting opportunities for the child to experience his or her own spoken language in written form. The child may begin by saying something about a picture she has drawn or a model she has constructed. The teacher or parent writes down the child's speech as a caption and the child may read it back, trace over it or copy it out. As confidence and ability grow, the child begins to undertake the task for herself and produces larger blocks of written language to pass on information or make up stories. It is easy to see that the secondary school child undertaking a piece of imaginative writing and the adult writing a letter to a friend are in essence both carrying out the same task as the young child copying out a caption. In all three cases thoughts are being organized in the form of language, carefully considered, and then set down on paper as an act of communication or a more permanent record.

Children's Words

Language-experience of this type has a great deal to offer in integrating the language arts. Its contribution and distinctive advantages can be divided up into the following categories:

- As the method is based on the child making the decision about what items he wants to communicate, the work stems from his own interests and as such is more likely to be viewed as meaningful and realistic. Purposes are set and the use of language is rescued from appearing as something imposed by the teacher for reasons little understood by the child.

- As the language originates with the child, he finds it easier to read back because it is made up of vocabulary and grammatical structures which are normal in his speech. The child thus learns that spoken language can be written down and then read back by himself and others. The child realizes that language is about communicating meaning and that written language gives permanence to his thoughts.

- The teacher is able to observe the level of the child's language development and by starting from the actual language of the child can stimulate further language growth and overcome any problems or lack of development of language understanding and use.

- The child learns the conventions of written language in association with his own spoken language and develops more helpful concepts of the terms we use to talk about language, such as word, sentence, letter and sound.

- As the composing of the written language is more thoughtful and deliberate than is the case with spoken language, more attention is paid to the message and to expressing it clearly.

- The child learns to identify words in a meaningful context and the importance of clear handwriting and accurate spelling are made more obvious.

It would seem, therefore, that *language-experience* provides the most natural introduction to the use of written language, makes provision for the integrated development of the language arts and enables the parent or teacher to undertake instruction on the basis of knowing the type and level of each child's spoken language development. But like all other methodologies it is not without its own problems and limitations.

- Some children resist the teacher's invitation to supply items of information which can be used as the basis of the activity. This can stem from a number of basic causes such as:

    (a) emotional insecurity
    (b) a wish to keep the teacher in ignorance of the child's life outside school
    (c) a lack of the kinds of experiences in the child's life which he or she wants to pass on to others
    (d) a fear that his or her language will not be acceptable
    (e) very poor language development.

- The teacher has the problem of providing the experiences to stimulate interest and producing from them the type of language-experience that each child is to need if he or she is to achieve steady language development. Unless this is done, the child is likely to resort to the security of producing over and over again only the content, vocabulary and grammatical structures which have proved acceptable in the past.

- The teacher must build up support in terms of instruction in handwriting and reference material to aid spelling.

- The work can become very much a one-way traffic, for all the language to be used comes in the first instance from the child. This makes it hard in the early stages to provide experience and materials which match the child's present language level but at the same time challenge him to expand his knowledge and use of language.

However, as already indicated, *language-experience* can be defined differently. John Merritt has pointed out that it may be looked upon in terms of experience which cannot be successfully completed without the use of language. For example, the adult who has lost his way may read a map, consult street names or ask some other person for directions. The adult must use language to achieve a satisfactory resolution. There will obviously be many opportunities throughout the school years where this type of method can be used to develop the use of language. The young child wishes to feed the classroom pet, so she must read the details of the amounts and kinds of food to be provided. The child may wish to bake a cake and so must consult a recipe. Perhaps it has been discovered that the children do not understand the school safety instructions, so the children may be asked to carry out a fire practice and then write fire drill instructions in their own words and display them in the classroom. Projects, topics and individual subjects form a basis for continuing this type of *language-experience*. The child needs to find information and process, collate, and memorize it and language must be the vehicle for achieving the desired result.

Sometimes, however, children are put in the situation where the intention is to provide for realistic use of language, but the reality is to make the children feel that written work is simply penalizing or checking up on them for the privilege of having had an enjoyable experience. Take, for instance, the common practice of going with children on a visit, say to the zoo. The experience has been enjoyed and has probably involved much stimulation and use of spoken language. Back in school, however, the children are instructed to write about the outing. The satisfactions of such an experience may quickly fade and sheer duty reporting will lack motivation. The whole event could still, of course, be turned into a realistic and satisfying project if the children were made to want to extend their knowledge, through using reference books or exchanging experiences by collating their information, giving it to another group of children and starting up a dialogue on the differences between two zoos. Perhaps the most useful subject for this *language-experience* method is that which starts with a study of the problems and possibilities of the local environment and society. For example, a class could study a wide range of topics from the provision for leisure activities and local employment prospects, to the possible effect of modern spraying techniques on health.

This second type of *language-experience* supplements the first in the following ways:

- It helps the teacher provide a wider range of possibilities for stimulating children to widen their knowledge, and challenges them to master and use new vocabulary and language structures.

- Whereas the first type of language-experience is helpful in creating opportunities to use language to convey personal information and/or communicate imaginative thinking, this second type involves children in the forms of language used to impart information and in the more transactional forms, such as instructions.

- The children practise, in realistic settings, using language to form purposes, select materials and set outcomes. This enables them to control their experiences and move further along the way to becoming independent thinkers and learners.

- Because such experiences often bring groups of children together, the teacher can overcome the largely individual approach of the first type of language experience and thus initiate the sharing of each individual's language abilities among the whole group.

Many of the aims set out earlier for teaching the language arts across the curriculum do seem to be accommodated by the joint use of these two groups of language-experience methods. Even so, there do remain a few problems. For *language-experience* can over-emphasize the everyday experience, stressing too much the more functional activities and on the use of language for handling information. This means neglecting the fantasy aspect of the child's life and that stimulation to thinking which comes from creative and imaginative types of task.

Equally, there is still the problem of how to aid the child's search for success in learning by structuring and planning the situations and materials with which he has to work. Whilst one would not want to narrow down the opportunities presented, the child's motivation for learning and using his own language will soon deteriorate if he is regularly faced with tasks or materials that are too difficult.

With these problems in mind we will now turn to the *story method*, which may help to provide a solution to the apparent language-experience limitations.

Story method

According to some recent studies of preschool children who had achieved a good level of reading ability, it was through the *story method* that the majority had learned. This is perhaps the oldest of the teaching reading methods and represents a very natural introduction to reading, once again involving the use of spoken language.

In its most primitive form, *story method* simply consisted of a child looking at the text whilst a story was read to him. When the story was one which was well-loved and oft-repeated, the child found that she could recognize words and phrases within the text. This form has recently been rediscovered in the USA as a remedial reading teaching method and rechristened the 'neurological impress

Approaches to language teaching

method'. In this approach the teacher reads to an individual child, the child is asked to join in and read together with the teacher, the latter gradually lowering the voice and omitting certain sections as the child gains in confidence. Then, to ensure that word learning is also taking place, echo techniques are used whereby the teacher reads out a word or phrase and the child is asked to point it out in the text as she reads it back. Quite rightly this will be regarded as a highly mechanical technique and one destined to give the child the impression that learning to read is about the memorization of words and not about the appreciation of meaning − a limitation already suggested as harmful to good development.

Fortunately many other versions of story method are available to the parent and teacher today; the most interesting of them are given below. They demonstrate the widening of the basic method and how it can be extended beyond the beginning stages of reading to play a full part in developing all the language arts. Later examples will demonstrate their use and extend these models.

1 The teacher can use the method even before written language is introduced, by telling a story in relation to a set of pictures only and asking a child, or preferably a group of children, to try to predict what will happen next. Afterwards, the children can be asked simply to put the pictures in the correct sequence or perhaps retell the story orally. Such retellings in the child's own language can form some of the early reading materials to be used at a later date by taping the child's story and transcribing it.

2 For very young children and those who are learning slowly or have language difficulties, it is best to use something which is very brief and has rhyme and rhythm such as nursery rhymes, jingles, jokes, limericks, television slogans, pop songs or simple hymns. The following steps have been found helpful:

(a) Provide a small group with a taped version which they may listen to as many times as they wish and let them discuss and attempt to memorize the text.

(b) Give the group a second taped version where some words, say the rhyming ones, have been deleted by the teacher and the children compete with each other to replace the omissions.

(c) Present this second tape and the complete text to each individual child so that he may read the whole with the challenge of remembering the omitted words sufficiently to recognize them within the text without the help of the teacher or another child. In practice the words omitted from the tape seem to be those which the children first manage to identify when they are asked to read words presented in isolation.

3 A story may be told to the children, perhaps more than once, followed by discussion and then by the children's own dramatization of it. Labels, such as names of characters and places, can be made and used by the actors. Alternatively puppets can be made: a puppet theatre increases the opportunity of introducing written language, for captions can be made to introduce events or set the scene. Using puppets often helps those children who, for some reason, rarely talk in discussions or are afraid to act in a normal play. As a conclusion to these activities, the children may individually read the original story to the teacher, tell a picture guided summary of it, or read the teacher's transcription of the dramatized version produced by the children.

4 As a change from the presented story, a small group of children can be given a starter statement such as 'It was dark, the wind was blowing strongly and suddenly the door blew open' or a situation, such as a road accident, and asked to create a story or play. In the early stages

these would be taped, transcribed by the teacher and then read by the children. At a later stage of development, the children can write them and then read or dramatize them for other groups of children. Children gain great enjoyment and a sense of success from presenting their work to others and especially to younger children.

5 Group prediction often helps to appreciate the construction of stories and gain the ability of viewing the text as a whole of which words, sentences, incidents and ideas are contributory parts. Here a story is divided into two or more episodes and after each episode has been read to them or they have read it silently, the children come together as a group to discuss how the story might continue and share the clues which they feel are important. After completing the story they return and reconsider any ideas they had which appear to have misled them and look again at the text to see if they can find the reasons for their misconceptions.

6 Activity (5) can be reversed to emphasize sequencing as well as prediction. This is done by giving the children crucial sentences from a short story in jumbled order and they consider in discussion the best order. They may then either create their own complete text before reading the author's version or use their order as a guide to study the author's text.

7 Activity (6) can also be used with subject texts. It has been found that many difficult concepts in subjects such as science are more clearly understood if children are set to discuss a jumbled version. Either a sentence with jumbled words or a paragraph of jumbled sentences is given and pairs of small groups of children work together to establish a satisfactory order.

When children have become familiar with discussion procedures in relation to story method over the years, their ability to appreciate literature is very much enhanced as is their ability to recognize bias and prejudice in media such as newspapers. Discussions of, say, characterization, atmosphere and style in a novel or play become highly successful and they become adept at recognizing the differing treatments of emotional and moral situations and ideas across a number of texts. Story method, then, has the following contributions to make:

- A series can be compiled which gives a skeleton structure for the work of a class, thus providing some control over challenging children excessively in terms of vocabulary and sentence structures. Carefully selected, the vocabulary and grammar can be closely related to what is likely to be children's spoken language ability in the early stages of school life.

- As the children mature, story method aids development by providing a wider range of vocabulary, language forms, styles and situations to stimulate further work and interests.

- The children always start from a basis which has meaning. Even if they cannot read all the words, they feel they have mastered the story line. Apart from aiding whole-word learning and the identification of words in terms of the grammatical and meaningful context, the method gives the child an understanding of the purpose of reading.

- All children share in the success. They always have the message even if they cannot remember all the words. For children who have learning difficulties the solution is relatively easy – more practice, not of the type of labouring through mechanical exercises but rather the presentation of further stories. The child learns to read by reading.

- Written and spoken language are used together thus

achieving some measure of integration of all the language arts and permitting learning in each of the aspects of language use to influence growth in the others.

- Thoughtful and meaningful usage of language is made the most of, the ability to follow and predict language and story sequences is encouraged and the children learn the importance of cause and effect relationships.

- It supplements language-experience methods by (a) introducing language forms and interests other than those which originate from the individual child; (b) providing for creative and imaginative experiences and uses of language to parallel the more everyday and functional usage of language.

A note on discussion

Much emphasis has been laid in recent years on the importance of individual differences and the special learning needs of each child. This has led to much more work being undertaken at the individual level especially among children with learning difficulties. However, individualization can be taken too far until it becomes a hindrance to the child's total development. So, whilst bearing in mind the importance of the careful study of each child's needs, abilities and learning styles, and using these as a basis for teaching, the limitations must also be recognized. Learning situations could well be limited to each child working only with materials and the teacher but not with other children. If a balance is sought between individual work and work in small groups, the availability of group work can bring the following extra advantages:

- a link is forged between the spoken and written uses of language and especially between language-experience and story method teaching approaches

Children's Words

- written language is seen as part of communication
- written language is no longer seen as being infallible
- training in social interaction and interpersonal relationships is possible
- the simplest steps forward in the expansion of vocabulary and grammatical knowledge are undertaken as the child's own language is usually nearer in type to that of his peers than to that of his teacher
- the child will reveal his or her own personal and language needs more freely, providing a wider frame for observation and understanding by the teacher. This is especially true in terms of the child's normal language usage and the development of his concepts of word meaning, which tend to be more obvious within group discussion than within individual conversations between teacher and child.

There are many occasions when the child will take part in conversations and informal group discussions, inside and outside the classroom. These have considerable value in terms of interaction and the general language development of the child. But they do suffer from two limitations. In the first place, since they are not usually observed by the teacher in any detail, they do not lend themselves to any detailed diagnostic analysis. And secondly, no framework is set in terms of developing language and its use. In order to gain such information for the teacher and for the child's own development, particular types of structured small group discussions are suggested as an important part of the methodology of language teaching (see chapter 3 for procedures for preparing and using appropriate materials).

Discussions may be structured in many ways, relating to material read by the children, or stories read to them, or picture sequences or starter statements and questions. The structure is set by having some clearly defined objective and by carefully selecting any required language or picture materials. Given such a basis, the teacher's directions and the children's sharing of their knowledge, thinking and language results in each child being able to develop his or her own insights and use of language. Once the children have had some practice in the various procedures, such discussions can take place without the teacher's presence, though some such discussions should be led by the teacher to further stimulate the children's thinking and to observe any needs which the children betray. It is also a good idea to taperecord the discussions occasionally so that the language behaviour of the children can be considered later away from the immediate pressures of the teacher's classroom responsibilities. In general terms structured discussions fall into two main types.

Cooperative discussion

The basis of this type consists in two or more children working together to seek some information or solution. Often it can be a part of subject or topic work as well as work based on individual textbooks or stories. As such it forms a part of both *language-experience* and *story method* approaches.

(a) Two children are given a sequence of pictures or sentences from a story or textbook in random order and discuss what is the most logical order in which they can be rearranged. In this activity young children can begin to learn the structure of stories, understand cause and effect relationships and learn how main and subordinate ideas in a text fit into a cohesive whole. While older children working on sections from textbooks clarify their concepts of technical vocabulary and learn the style of writing and thinking expecially appropriate to each subject area. For example, the accepted form of writing up scientific experiments with the heavy usage of the passive voice which children use little in conversation.

(b) The use of cloze procedure, i.e. the presentation of a text from which words have been omitted, can present a useful base for discussion in either story or informational type material. In endeavouring to select the most appropriate words to complete the text the children must comprehend the text, making use of syntactic and semantic cues. Through discussing which words from their spoken vocabulary stores are most appropriate, attention is drawn to the variable meanings which can be associated with individual words and their level of appropriateness in terms of the meaning of the passage and the style of writing used by the author.

(c) Stories may be divided into serial episodes and discussions held after each separate episode where the children are challenged to predict how the story will continue. The episodes can be based on pictures, stories read to children, or stories where the children read each episode silently before the discussion. (Prediction plays a large part in the success of both listening and reading activities. The adult, when listening or reading, builds up an expectancy of how the originator of the language is going to continue and checks his prediction against the flow of language which follows. In this way the listener or reader becomes actively involved, marshalling his own knowledge, thinking and purposes in order to interpret the new information being passed to him.)

Comparative discussions

In this type of discussion children combine and compare information after having collected material from different sources. For example, different versions of the same event can be studied with the discussion aimed at establishing what the facts really are and what influences have caused versions to draw rather different cause and effect relations or bias their account in a particular way. In historical studies, for example, the accounts of the events occurring during the French Revolution as set out in British and French textbooks could be compared. Daily newspapers provide a good source for the comparative study of current affairs. It is often helpful to such discussions to assist the children in their search by giving starter questions or making them analyse the material read by modelling devices such as flow diagrams or matrices prior to the discussions. Such discussions help to both widen the children's thinking and deepen their understanding of the complexity of meaning and the detection of bias and prejudice.

An integrated approach to the teaching of the language arts

Language learning, it has been argued, is far more likely to be successful if undertaken in an integrated manner in relation to the total curriculum. Yet even this approach is not without its pitfalls:

- Some elements of the language arts may be given more attention than others, thus possibly creating an imbalance of development among the children.
- The teacher and children become so involved in the projects that the language objectives are forgotten and opportunities for skill development missed.
- It is often difficult to ensure a structure for each individual child's learning.
- Among older children the demands of a content-centred curriculum and timetabling can often make it difficult to plan a holistic programme.

The discussion and examples that follow attempt to create an atmosphere and framework to overcome these difficulties as far as is possible. Chapter 3 presents advice on the diagnostic frameworks which, used in support of the general approach, should ensure that the individual child's language needs are also fulfilled.

When linked together in a single teaching approach

An integrated teaching approach

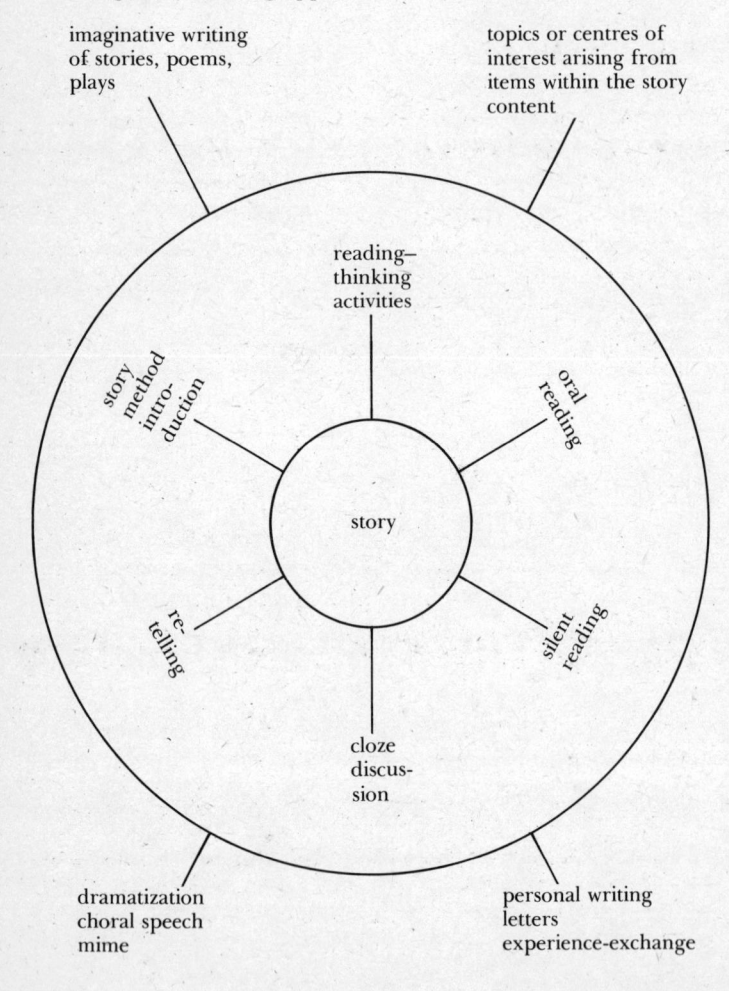

imaginative writing of stories, poems, plays

topics or centres of interest arising from items within the story content

- reading–thinking activities
- story method introduction
- oral reading
- story
- re-telling
- silent reading
- cloze discussion

dramatization
choral speech
mime

personal writing
letters
experience-exchange

Approaches to language teaching

language-experience and *story method* not only offer an opportunity to involve all the language arts in relation to a curriculum content but allow the teacher to plan in advance the general language objectives and structure of learning. Given this general framework, the needs of the child can be observed and modifications made to ensure that the learning is appropriate. Whereas many teaching programmes are devised with a view to learning certain skills and then suggest that further practice is given in the use of skills, I suggest that the teacher builds a programme from experiences which seem to offer value and interest to children at a given stage of development. Such experiences also provide for the widest possible range of language functions and processes. The point of departure is therefore subject matter and experiences which are valuable to the children for their own sake but which in their completion give the opportunity to develop language learning.

Though spoken language develops before the use of written language, the more permanent and accessible nature of written language makes it easier for the teacher, as well as the parents, to preplan and structure a programme for the language arts based upon written materials. This central material forms a nucleus from which the children may commence and expand their experiences and uses of language. In the figure opposite the nucleus of a story is encircled by possible treatments of it and radiating from it are further possibilities for imaginative and informational activities which can involve written and/or spoken language.

A reservation to the integrated approach

The approach to the development of the language arts outlined so far is capable of including all but the mastery of two aspects of growth in the use of language. The two exceptions are handwriting and spelling. The explanation for this is that these two areas are of a much more mechanical nature than all the others and are not learned effectively without the undertaking of very specific activities. As they are mechanistic it is best if the child is helped to master them early. In this way worries about handwriting and spelling do not absorb mental energy, thus distracting the child from a full concentration upon the meaning he wishes to transmit. It is a common enough experience to see children, especially those from the high and low ability ranges, lose the thread of the idea that they wish to express whilst framing the letter shapes or hesitating over the spelling of a word. This problem is certainly not solved by encouraging children to ignore handwriting and spelling. Such a course leads only to greater confusion in the future – a confusion which affects other areas of language development as well as handwriting and spelling.

Handwriting

At the very beginning of school life and again at a later stage if some form of cursive writing is introduced, it is helpful if the child is directed towards the most economic form of letter construction. When this is carefully undertaken the confusion of letters, their reversal, e.g. 'b' for 'd', or their inversion, e.g. 'n' for 'u' is reduced not only in writing but also in reading. The amount of time taken by the mechanical work in letter construction in the very early stages will be small but most rewarding for both children and teacher. The following procedures are helpful:

1 Tracing with the finger over felt or sandpaper letters. It is important that the child is not given the opportunity to consolidate bad habits by tracing over the letters in a haphazard manner. Perhaps the best method of achieving consistency is to mark each letter with a green dot where the child must commence and a red dot where the construction of the letter should be completed. The direction of the movement should be

Approaches to language teaching

bd

indicated by arrows. For children who find a good deal of practice necessary, 'writing' letters with their fingers on each other's backs or in the air gives a variation to the activity.

2 Once the child appears to have a good idea of the movement involved in constructing letters, tracing over letters which are presented in the form of dots or broken lines can be commenced. At this point, lines should be included for sequence and position in space needs to be established – the child who undertakes his early writing experiences on unlined paper is at an obvious disadvantage, as is also the child who lacks some direction as to how letters should be placed in relation to each other. The best form of lined paper is that which gives the child guidance concerning comparative size and position, e.g.

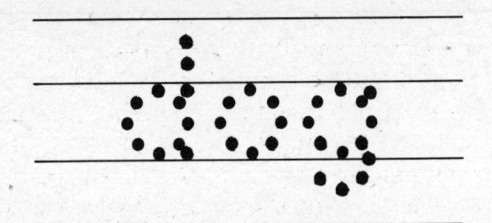

The appropriate use of capital and lower case letters should be introduced early or this too adds to future confusion. It is important that captions and notices in the classroom should have the correct form, and that notices are not displayed which are all in block capitals or sentences written which do not commence with a capital letter. The child who writes his name as 'pAul' is usually a product of a teaching situation where capitals have been introduced haphazardly and consistent responses have not been demanded. The writing of the child's own name gives one of the first opportunities to establish rules and good habits.

In what order letter shapes are introduced must be left to the individual teacher. Those who feel that the visual and motor development of the children is of great importance tend to classify the letters according to the shape to be constructed. This means that letters of vertical lines are introduced first, then those with circles, followed by those constructed from a mixture of the two and finally, those which have partial forms, e.g. 'h'. The teacher who uses a whole word approach to reading, on the other hand, usually introduces letters in alphabetical order whereas the teacher who concentrates partially upon phonic instruction tends to introduce all the vowels first and then consonants in the order most likely to produce high numbers of words in the early stages, e.g. from the vowels and p, t and s, almost every combination produces an English word which is phonically simple.

Approaches to language teaching

3 The next stage is the copying of sentences underneath the teacher's writing on the same piece of paper. It is at this stage that the children have to learn the nature of letter and word boundaries. Some children are helped by using such devices as placing a finger at the end of each word before commencing the first letter of a new word. The child is helped to achieve knowledge of word boundary if the sentence is read in unison with the teacher several times and the child is asked to point to the beginning of each new word at it is spoken.

As has already been shown, the attention the child needs to give to the motor task of writing and spelling in the early stages can inhibit his ability to present the ideas and information he wishes to impart. What appears to happen is that he cannot hold the meaning he has framed long enough to set it down on paper. It would seem helpful, therefore, to divide the two parts of the task until the child is more proficient. This can be achieved by tape recording any information or ideas he wishes to impart and then allowing him to use the pause button on a cassette player to write down his recorded work one word at a time. At a later stage it is helpful if the child produces a fair copy of his free writing for display purposes where the teacher has helped him to correct any mistakes made in the original.

Spelling

Spelling accuracy is important for efficient written communication and its mastery does have some small feedback support to the development of reading. However, the correlation between reading and spelling attainment is low – the child does not become good at spelling as a result of being a fluent reader. Although it has often been urged that spelling and phonics can helpfully be taught together, this seems a doubtful approach. After all, the rules which govern English spelling are so many – hardly surprising given the many other languages on which English draws – and at the end of the day the rules are far from foolproof. Given the further inconsistencies of the sound/symbol relationships, then the system presents an impossible task to the learner. Seemingly the most helpful approach to learning spelling is to concentrate upon the memorization of visual sequences and to erect rules only on the basis of a number of examples already known to the child. Editing and successive drafting are respectable (indeed essential) adult writing activities often denied children.

With any new word the child wishes to master, the following procedure should be adopted:

1 Look carefully at the word
2 Close eyes and try to visualise it
3 Think whether it has any unusual features, special or irregular features which distinguish it from other words
4 Write it out once without looking at the original copy
5 Always check the attempt against the original
6 Go through the whole procedure again if the attempt does not match the original

A word of warning: the practice of writing a word out five or ten times as an aid to memorization seems fraught with difficulty. It parallels the situation where a child learning the piano is given a new piece of music, is shown the most efficient fingering procedure and then goes away and practises for a week. Without extra guidance, however, mistakes in fingering might creep in and these will be consolidated by practice. In the same way the child who is allowed to continue practising a spelling error consolidates the learning of the error which becomes more difficult to eradicate than it was to teach it effectively in the first instance.

The presentation of lists of words to children for them to learn only seems effective if they are words which the child needs to use. Equally it is better if the child learns to spell a word before he uses it in his written work than as a correction after his written work is completed. Though obviously not always possible incorrect spellings can be restricted if a good support system is built up in the classroom and the children are encouraged to use it freely.

It is common practice in infant schools for children to compile personal picture dictionaries or word books and at later stages for the use of published dictionaries to be introduced. My own preference at the primary stage is for the building up of group or class word banks. These give a greater flexibility of usage and are cooperative rather than individual in compilation. Thus the vocabulary of the whole group is a stimulus to the growth of the individual and the children find such word banks more fun. The design possibilities of word banks are very wide but I have found commercially produced punched card systems are the easiest to handle and are more durable than the use of small pieces of thin card. An expensive cabinet is not essential as a shoe box with one narrow end cut so that it falls forward when the lid is removed is adequate.

In the case of very young or older less able children, the listing of words associated with one topic on a single card is helpful. The children can then look at the list of topics and push in the needle at the appropriate spot and the relevant card will be selected which they wish to consult or indeed, add to the list of words on that topic. With older and more able children it is best to have an alphabetical arrangement.

Sub-classifications can then be built up by punching holes on the sides of the cards to cover items such as the following which will be seen to have benefits as a resource for written work, spelling, vocabulary expansion and phonic teaching:

- alphabetical classification
- rhyming words
- common phonic patterns
- words with similar meanings
- words which are frequently confused
- parts of speech

Children's Words

It is not uncommon to find both parents and teachers challenging a child for a spelling error when the mistake has not been made as the result of inability to spell a word. Since the spelling of English words is influenced by grammar and meaning it is frequently the case that the child's difficulty is to be located in these areas rather than in spelling *per se*. The teacher has to ensure that the cause of the error is clearly understood. The child who confuses 'there' and 'their' is unlikely to do so as a spelling difficulty. Much more likely is it that he does not understand the significance in grammar and meaning which they symbolize. On the other hand when 'their' is written as 'thier' the signalling of spelling confusion is more likely.

As the child grows in language development a dictionary will become a valuable aid. Features which are particularly useful to the child are a clear system of pronunciation of the words and the listing of similar words rather than long lists of definitions which may confuse. In fact a thesaurus which lists words of the same or similar uses would appear to be of more value than a dictionary at the primary stage and is useful alongside a dictionary at the secondary stage. When selecting either, one should particularly examine whether or not the volume ensures that words used in the lists or definitions also appear as main headings.

The approach and children with language difficulties

The traditional approach to the diagnosis of learning difficulties, as we saw in chapter 1, was to identify what was a child's level of attainment and, by comparison with what was seen to be average behaviour, to look for specific weaknesses. It seemed natural, therefore, that attempts to help such children should commence with work in subskill areas where the children appeared to have weaknesses. Such approaches have long been challenged and a large number of research studies into work in the field of remedial educa-

Approaches to language teaching

tion have suggested that in the long term they were ineffective. Ineffective in that even when the children showed improvement they tended to regress later as a result of a failure to re-establish good attitudes towards reading as an activity. Significant factors were undoubtedly:

- the children's worry at being asked to work heavily in the areas of their greatest weakness
- the children often failed to understand the relevance and nature of the tasks they were asked to undertake and so found it hard to become highly motivated
- the activities did not seem to demonstrate that any worthwhile success was being achieved

All this is not to say that children do not have specific language difficulties or that in certain cases extra practice in some of the subskills will be necessary. The essential point is that if we are to overcome any lag in development or difficulty a child has, it becomes even more important that the work given emphasizes the reality, usefulness and enjoyment of language activities.

The old model could be represented as follows:

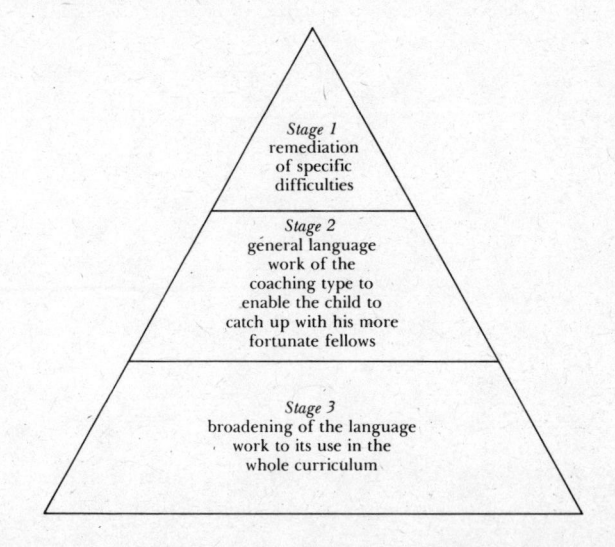

Stage 1
remediation of specific difficulties

Stage 2
general language work of the coaching type to enable the child to catch up with his more fortunate fellows

Stage 3
broadening of the language work to its use in the whole curriculum

This diagram shows clearly that the child has no real opportunity to apply his learning realistically until the final stage of the remedial work. If the worries voiced earlier about the teaching of isolated subskills and the ease with which the teacher can be deceived by an initial diagnosis have any substance, then work in Stages 1 and 2 may not only be inappropriate, but increase resistant attitudes and thus fail to ever get the child to Stage 3.

A more acceptable model is offered by the following diagram which suggests that in the basic teaching approach little difference is needed in type from that suggested earlier as a general model. Expressed more firmly, no single approach appears to be more helpful than any other to the child with language difficulties. Instead of a special approach remedial teaching only requires a teacher with a watchful eye, considerable insight into childrens' needs and a wider range of activities to enable the slower child to consolidate the learning.

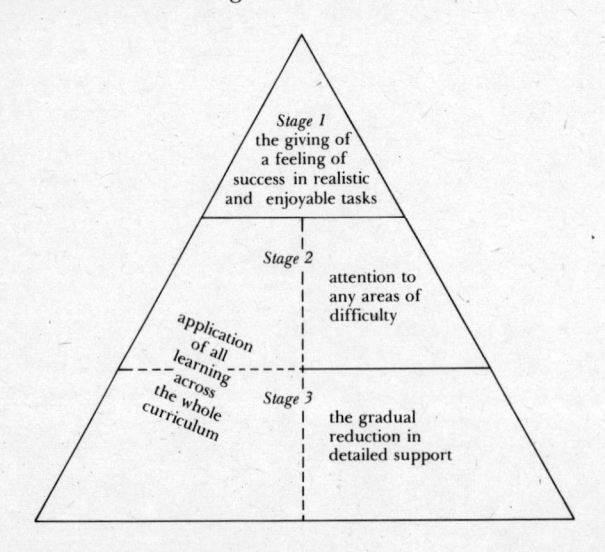

Stage 1 the giving of a feeling of success in realistic and enjoyable tasks

Stage 2 attention to any areas of difficulty

application of all learning across the whole curriculum

Stage 3 the gradual reduction in detailed support

Here the sole emphasis of Stage 1 is to ensure that the child gains some success in the area or areas of language activity

Approaches to language teaching

where she appears to have difficulties. The aim is to reorientate attitudes towards the task, restore the child's self-image as a learner, allow time for counselling concerning her personal worries and ensure that any observation of needs is undertaken in an atmosphere where the child is working on a meaningful task and motivated to succeed. In this way the teacher is more likely to find real needs rather than a wider range of possible needs which may be only the generalization of a sense of failure.

The various forms of story method, language-experience and discussion techniques would seem ideal for achieving this success-giving exercise for between them they emphasize meaning, realism and the worthwhileness of communication. Each also allows for considerable repetition but does so in an atmosphere where meaning is still paramount in the eyes of the child.

Stage 2 continues from this but supplemented where necessary to combat any gaps in learning, delays in development or specific difficulties which the individual child may have. This secondary area may be referred to as supplementary teaching and it is envisaged as taking place in the form described in Merritt's GPID model (see pp. 37–8). Thus the child within a normal language activity will realize or be helped to realize his need to master certain processes or skills so that when he enters the implementation phase he is enabled to achieve the desired outcomes to satisfy his needs in the most effective manner possible. Such supplementary teaching could virtually be in any area but the most common fall into the following general areas:

- inadequate perceptual skills
- lack of vocabulary
- weaknesses of grammatical usage
- lack of comprehension skills
- inadequate development of word attack skills
- inability to follow a logical argument
- lack of knowledge of study techniques
- weaknesses in spelling

Such detailed support can easily place children in a situation of some dependency upon the teacher despite the fact that it is undertaken in relation to realistic activities and arising from the meaningful setting of the whole curriculum. Just as a plant raised in greenhouse conditions will wilt if suddenly faced with the temperature and humidity variations outside, so the child who has undergone a period of protection and expansion needs to have time for gradual readjustment before he can be totally independent as a language learner. For this purpose Stage 3 is inserted where the child is weaned towards independent thinking and learning.

The above model appears to cover more than 99 per cent of children who experience any form of language learning difficulty. The exceptions appear to be those who have a blockage of some sensory or perceptual channel. This minute group need to have some compensatory mechanism, e.g. the use of braille or the optacon for the child who is blind. Some children in this category who, though they have no obvious physical defect, experience such difficulty in one of the perceptual areas that compensatory teaching is necessary. For example a child who has very low development in the visual perception area may be helped by being given experiences through the senses of touch and movement combined with discussion to establish concepts of size, shape, texture and position. The language used within such discussion helps to establish concepts which can then be used in the development of visual perception.

Examples of the general approach in action

The following examples are aimed to demonstrate the use of language experience and story method jointly within an integrated language across the curriculum approach. Obviously, within the limits of this book, space is not available to present a total programme even if that was desirable – for the interests and needs of children will vary from school to school and class to class as will also the enthusiasm of the teacher and the resources in the school environment. All these matters influence the type of activity which will be of most value.

The examples have been selected to demonstrate how the approach might be used with children of a variety of ages and levels of attainment. Deliberately they have been chosen to cover a wide range of interests, and different starting points, thus providing opportunities for the development of a variety of language skills and processes. In each example the major types of learning involved are clearly outlined. The teacher, in designing similar activities, is reminded that it is important to study the various activities over a period of time to ensure that together they are forming an appropriate diet of language learning opportunities. For it is all too easy to use activities which are overly similar in terms of the language development they create. When this happens the child develops an imbalance which may restrict his use of language in the environment outside the school or may even make development difficult at some future stage. For example if activities concentrated heavily upon the processing of information, then the development of the expressive and imaginative forms of language would be unduly neglected. Equally, at a lower level the use of context could be emphasized in word identification to the exclusion of development of phonic skills.

Example One *Fluffy's Aeroplane*
A survey of the material available for the development of reading readiness reveals that much of it aims to develop readiness via activities in the areas of the separate perceptual skills. Some few more recent materials concentrate on the development of spoken vocabulary. Looking at most of the published readiness tests we find sections on visual perception and left/right orientation, auditory perception, letter recognition and vocabulary. Research, however, has

Children's Words

Approaches to language teaching

demonstrated that the results of such tests have a very low level of prediction of future success, and the subsections are not even very revealing in terms of the diagnosis of children's real needs. If such test materials are open to these criticisms, then similar types of learning activities may be less than efficient in encouraging a good start on the reading process.

Let us now briefly discuss how picture books may be used for integrated language arts work at the readiness or pre-reading stage. The material used is drawn from the Kate and Fluffy Books (Language Patterns). Each of these books presents stories as a basis for small group discussion where the diagnosis of individual needs and the experience to satisfy such needs are undertaken together.

This illustration is taken from *Fluffy's Aeroplane*, a fantasy story concerning the use of Fluffy's magic bell to change the boy's birthday from its unhappy start into a day of exciting adventures. This is how it should be studied.

1 The first stage is to ensure that all the children recognize and can supply a name label for each of the elements in the illustration. This gives the opportunity to observe general knowledge, ensure that children can recognize the two-dimensional representation of the three-dimensional world of their experience and have the vocabulary to apply to the objects.

2 The discussion then moves on with the teacher asking questions to probe more deeply into the nature of the relationships and the situation described in the illustration. Basically the task is for the children to discover the messages the illustrator is trying to communicate. The teacher will be stimulating the discussion by asking questions such as 'Why are there so many toys lying on the floor?', 'Do you think the children are happy, sad or bored?', 'Why do you think they are sad?', 'What is Fluffy doing?', 'Why are they all looking out of the window?'

At this stage the children are learning the meaning and form of 'wh' questions [why, what, where, which, when], phrasing answers in sentence form and learning the use of various parts of speech. Items such as 'top', 'bottom', 'left', 'right' give useful practice in the use of books in terms of the reversal of the anatomical positions and a first step towards the mastery of the special importance of orientation in the English writing system. Many young children are uncertain of the precise meanings of prepositions. In this particular picture the recognition of the meaning, implied by the rain, is important and some children show uncertainty as to whether it is raining inside and outside. The first explanation of this was looked for in some failing in the illustration itself but this has not proved to be the case. The problem appeared to lie in the inadequate development of the concepts of meaning signalled by the words 'inside' and 'outside'. The children only resolved the difficulty fully by running in and out of the classroom during a heavy shower.

Many children have difficulty in unifying the parts of a picture into one whole meaningful message and thereby recognizing the illustrator's main idea. Others centre their attention upon certain elements but ignore others and so again miss the main intent. By helping the children to recognize the overall meaning of an illustration the teacher sets the scene for the growth of the processes for recognizing the cohesive nature of text and appreciation of the way in which the elements combine to form the message a writer wishes to impart.

3 The final stage of the group discussion is to establish possible cause and effect relationships, e.g. Why do you think the children are fed up?, What do you think will happen now Fluffy has rubbed his bell?. In this picture the children may suggest that e.g. the children are on holiday and are sad they cannot go out to play.

Approaches to language teaching

It is Peter's birthday and he wants to play with his new football.
Fluffy wants to go for a walk.
It will stop raining and they will go out to play.
Fluffy's magic bell will make it stop raining.

The teacher must encourage the children to supply as many cause and effect relationships as possible for in understanding both written and spoken language, the mind builds up a frame of expectancy and predicts from the known into likely possibilities.

4 As each new page is met the above procedures are undertaken and past predictions discussed to see if there were clues to what would happen which had been missed or misunderstood. In this way, the cohesion of the whole message of the book begins to be recognised.

5 Up to this stage the work has used only oral language in response to the picture. However, when the discussion of the whole book is completed the first stages of written language can be employed. The children are asked to agree a story line for each page and, having done so, record it on tape. The teacher, or an older child, makes a transcription of this tape and then using a jumbo typewriter the text is set out and appended to each page. The children can then have a first reading experience by listening to their tape whilst looking at the written form. Usually they wish to do this many times and by doing so will almost inevitably memorize the written form of at least some words from their story.

Clearly language-experience and story method have worked together to give the children their first experience of print. The story is already known and the language forms used are those proposed by the children so there should not be any mismatch as so often occurs when the child meets the language of reading schemes as a first reading experience.

In the case of *Fluffy's Aeroplane* the possibilities for follow up work are very wide. Some which have been selected by children to date are:

Birthdays: histograms were made of the months in which the children in the class had their birthdays. Each was given a small square of gummed coloured paper and stuck it on a chart divided into twelve columns.

The children drew pictures to which name labels were supplied of the presents they had received on their last birthday.

The children discussed the type of treat they would most like on their next birthday.

Some children recounted their experiences on their last birthday and others discussed the sort of thing which would be exciting for Fluffy to do on his birthday.

Aeroplanes: the children collected pictures of different types of aeroplane.

Some children who had gone on holiday by air tried to explain the sensations of flying to the others.

Zoos and Circuses: The children collected pictures of animals and circus acts and described them to the group.

Obviously it would be stretching interest in the book too far to try and undertake all the above with any one group of children. One should try to capitalize on the ones which appear to hold most interest for the group or the follow-up work will appear stilted and thus lose impetus. However, for a short period the book could become the basis of the whole curriculum, giving opportunity for imaginative and informational uses of language in relation to a number of topics. All the stories and pieces of information should be transcribed, displayed and used as reading material, and the words used should form the basis of the group's word bank.

Approaches to language teaching

Introducing a reading scheme

The integrated approach outlined earlier could be used with most reading schemes but it is obviously easier if the scheme has been written with a story method approach in mind. The following are examples based upon three such schemes.

Example Two *Jack and Jill*

In the early stages even a short story is very often too long to enable the children to memorize the text sufficiently well for the learning to be efficient. Rhymes, jingles, jokes, pop songs and advertizing slogans provide shorter texts plus the extra aid to memorization of rhyme and rhythm. The following procedures, for example, were used for the rhyme 'Jack and Jill went up the hill'.

1 Illustrations were provided for the following stages within the rhyme:

> the two children climbing up the hill with the pail
> the children filling the pail at the well
> Jack falling
> Jill falling with Jack shown further down the slope
> Jack running home
> Jack in bed

The children discussed the pictures and then sequenced them in the appropriate order. Inevitably at this point the children question what happened to Jill and various suggestions will be given. The sequencing activity gives the children the idea of a left to right direction as they arrange the pictures in comic strip format. Cause and effect relationships have to be considered in order to put the pictures in a logical order and thus the children learn the importance of the chronological order of happenings within a story.

2 The story was discussed in terms of the historic impor-

Children's Words

tance of wells, how we now get our water and how different injuries might be treated.

3 The children were then given a taped version of the rhyme where the language was interspersed by various sound effects and this was listened to and enjoyed several times, the children being invited to join in and so commence the memorization of the rhyme. Here the children were meeting the vocabulary and more formal grammatical constructions of the rhyme and realizing the nature of rhyme and rhythm.

4 A second tape was given to the children where certain of the rhyming words were omitted and the children in the group competed to be the first to supply the missing words.

5 The children then were given an illustrated written version of the rhyme together with the tape from which words had been omitted to work with individually. They were directed to follow the words as the voice on the tape spoke them. Here the children were recognizing written versions of the spoken words, developing the understanding of the functions of letters and the nature of word boundaries. The children were allowed to continue with this activity as long as they wished. Normally this stage was ended by a child saying that he wanted to read the rhyme to the teacher without the help of the tape.

6 Follow-up work on the comprehension of the content and the memorization was subsequently pursued but many children did not need to undertake all the activities in order to be able to read the rhyme independently and memorize some of the words. (It is unwise at this stage to spoil the enjoyment and sense of success the children achieve by insisting that all the words must be memorized before moving on to other written language experiences.)

Approaches to language teaching

In the follow-up work:

a. The children were given the original illustrations and the text cut up into sections to sequence the two together. Some slower children needed to have a copy of the complete rhyme in order to do this at first.
b. The children were then asked to sequence the text without the help of illustrations or a copy of the whole text.
c. The above two activities were also undertaken with the rhyme cut up into single words as this is found helpful in giving children an understanding of the nature of words which will later be of great value to their identification and use.

Example Three *The Big Red Lorry*
This occupied the whole of an infant school reception class, though the subgroups of children within the class took different routes through the activities. The slower children undertook more of those concerned with the reader while the brighter ones spent rather more time on the follow-up and extension activities.

1 The introduction to the material followed the form which has been described above under Example One. The story line here concerns a red lorry which travels across the countryside occasionally dropping part of its load of pots and pans which later become homes for farm and wild animals. At the end of this section the children listened to their own taped version of the stories whilst they turned the pages of the picture book which was put together by cutting out the illustrations and remounting them in a book without any of the text.

2 The whole class then combined to make masks for the characters and models to represent the lorry and the

countryside. These were to form the basis for the dramatization of the story in company with the tape and later for free dramatization. At this stage the use of written language was introduced in the form of teacher-produced badges of the character names. (This also led to a project based upon the names of the children in the class.)

3 The group-produced stories were transcribed by the teacher and attached to the set of pictures. The children were given these to read with the help of the tape they had earlier produced.

4 The teacher then provided a dramatic telling of the author's version of the story with the children helping by providing the sound effects.

5 The children then read the author's version and drew pictorial maps to show the happenings.

6 The group discussed the items and happenings of the story again and set to work on two types of activity:

  a. to create their own poems and stories inspired by the book. The topics varied widely with the adventures of a lorry driver being the most popular as the red lorry in the particular illustration is driverless. The most popular efforts at poetic writing were related to pots and pans as they gave the children considerable possibility in terms of rhyme. All the efforts were finally tape recorded, transcribed by the teacher or older children and then illustrated by the originator. Each child then read his story or poem to the group and the work was placed in the book corner for later usage by other children. It was significant here how often the author of a story went to help another child read it.

  b. The class formed into groups and worked upon a variety of topics which were aimed to relate the

Approaches to language teaching

subject matter of the reader to everyday life experiences. The various topics covered were as follows:

Lorries – this group made a collection of pictures of a wide variety of lorries and classified them into various sets in accordance with the type of work for which they were designed. A count was undertaken of the numbers of each type of vehicle which passed the school and two histograms were made, one showing the numbers of each type seen, the other the total numbers of lorries passing the school in half-hour periods during the course of the school day. The material was labelled, displayed and the group talked about their work to the rest of the class.

Wild animals – a further group commencing with the animals used in the books and adding others to the list, collected pictures of them and with the teacher's help labelled and displayed them. They then searched information books for pictures of the types of home each lived in and were helped to find the parts of the world in which they lived.

Farm animals – pictures of farm animals were collected and labelled and the children discovered the various foods which they produced or the work they undertook for us. Illustrations of the animals at work and the processes in the production of such items as cheese were either drawn or made from pictures collected from magazines.

Pots and pans – illustrations of various types of cooking utensils were collected and labelled and captions made concerning their uses. Various types of cakes were baked, the recipes set out in flow diagram form and histograms constructed to show the popularity among the class of various types of cake.

In all the above activities the children expanded their knowledge, vocabulary and ability to communicate and learned several devices for the representation of information.

7 For those children who were not ready to continue to the next stage of the scheme, a similar treatment was given to the poem about a little engine which struggles with a heavy load. This poem has a not dissimilar vocabulary to the *Big Red Lorry* and allows for the same joint use of story method, language-experience and discussion.

Throughout all the stages the teacher created a word bank. Each of the important items such as lorry, the various animals, hills, etc. was provided with a card topped with an appropriate illustration. On the card were added words with explanatory pictures which the author or the children had used in relation to them. This proved a most helpful resource during the time the children were making their first attempt to create the written form of language.

Example Four *In the Village*
This reading scheme is built around the adventures of the various characters living in a village and the publishers supply materials to build a model of the village in the classroom.

1 Using the model, the children can engage in dramatic play creating their own spontaneous village happenings. Experience shows that often the children will ask that they may record or even write some of the work which arises from this situation.

2 The early books in this reading scheme permit the teacher to considerably expand the text given and make up very enjoyable stories to tell to the children. This expansion, however, must be carefully related to the illustrations and the given text, being clearly seen

as a summary of the story the children hear. After having heard the story the children, guided by their memory of the story line and the illustrations, read the text in the books.

3 It has proved helpful to use the early books as prediction exercises where the children discuss what may happen after reading each page.

4 The characters in the story are distinguished by the colour of their hats as well as their occupations and personalities. This use of colour as a distinguishing mark enables the establishment of names and certain of the most used words of the language. One approach which has proved successful with less able children and those learning English as a second language has been to make a booklet for each character where each page has a line illustration of the character. On each new page just one part of the illustration is coloured alongside a one sentence caption. The child quickly catches on to the idea that the colour used and the object coloured will appear in the sentence caption, e.g. 'His hat is blue', 'He has a black dog'.

Most value is obtained from these small booklets if chatty tapes are prepared which discuss the picture, the colours, the character of the person illustrated, the object coloured and occasionally the sounds in the words. The last task in respect of each page becomes the reading of the caption together with the voice on the tape.

Example Five *Lucy Maud Montgomery*
(A brief version of the life of the author of *Anne of Green Gables*. Age of children: 10+)
The story was read silently in episodes, each episode being followed by a group prediction discussion. Prediction in this case was not in terms of what would happen next, but rather what decision Lucy would take about her shyness and lone-

liness, her many refusals by publishers to publish her poems and stories, whether to become a teacher or a journalist, etc. This led to considerable discussion concerning emotions, feelings and the way in which decisions are made.

The children invented situations and asked their colleagues to say how they would make their decisions in relation to the problems. The teacher suggested the use of matrices and decision trees as aids to gaining clarity. For example a matrix listing the different models of bicycles on one dimension, and the essential features desired on the other, was constructed and used to collate information from brochures. As Lucy Montgomery's writing originated from a newspaper report of an adoption, the children tried to list all the questions they felt should be asked concerning an adoption and arranged them in a logical order with a decision tree.

Consequently, the topic led to practical help being given at a local children's home and to correspondence with children's societies for information about adoption and fostering.

When the children were challenged to write about the central situations, they produced stories and poems mainly concerned with the emotions of shyness, loneliness and rejection. In this case the challenge was that Lucy had sent off her first story to a publisher when she was only nine and the children were now ten or eleven. This task made a contribution to the children's ability to employ figurative language and work in the more abstract area of feelings and emotions.

Lucy's success as a journalist turned attention to the local newspaper, which the children felt was uninteresting. Following discussion, the children divided into interest groups, selecting areas which they felt would be useful to investigate. Some acted as reporters and others as editors and illustrators and for a few weeks the class produced a paper of local news.

This gave the children considerable insight into the format of and reading skills necessary to appreciate the content of a newspaper. They learned how to separate main and subordinate ideas, to select appropriate headlines, to write economically and make decisions concerning the sort of impact they wished to have. Some children developed skills of scanning and proof reading and all learned a great deal about the art of summarization.

Finally, without any pressure from the teacher, every member of the class read *Anne of Green Gables* and requested time to discuss their impressions of the story within the class.

The range of written language media the children engaged in within this project – fiction, biography, letters, brochures, pamphlets, newspapers – is particularly interesting. Too frequently classroom reading is heavily weighted in favour of books and children do not realise the different approaches to reading which can be demanded by the author's writing style and intentions. Again, at the onset of adolescence, children should be given the opportunity to explore the language of feelings and emotions, engage in fantasy exploration of them and be involved in decision making.

Example Six *An Environmental Study*
(carried out at the Meadows Primary School, Duffield. Age of children: 10 — 11+)

This project, worked upon by a whole class, arose from the observation early in the spring by one child that most of the plants in the hedgerows were dying. The class discussed this and decided that it may have been caused by salting the roads during winter. The children carried out experiments on the school field but found that the effect of the salt on vegetation was minimal. One child suggested that it might be due to the use of sprays, so it was decided to write to the County Surveyor to find out if this might be the case. All the children drafted a letter and then the class discussed which was the best in terms of politeness, clarity of the request for information and the appropriate form of address. It was

Children's Words

then decided to send the same letter to all county surveyors in England.

When the replies came many provided detailed information concerning the methods of controlling vegetation on verges, the heavy costs of cutting as against spraying, the timing of cutting or spraying and the various brands of weed killer which were used. This information was charted in various ways, e.g. piegraphs to show the methods of control used by the authorities, maps to show in which areas sprays were used and histograms to show the timing of cutting and spraying. The children became quite adept at extracting the appropriate information but many of the names of the weed killers and chemicals were unknown to them. They tried to identify these by visits to the library and to the science department of the local secondary school. There still remained a few items and so the children wrote to the manufacturers of the weed killers and also obtained the booklet from the Ministry of Agriculture which listed and described permitted sprays.

At this point two matters arose. Firstly the realization that farmers and market gardeners used such sprays and so one group wrote requesting information from them. Secondly it was noted that there were important discrepancies between the information given in the brochures from chemical companies and the Ministry of Agriculture leaflet. So a further group set about questioning officials and writing to companies again for further information. For example, one spray professed to include an effective fire depressant but it became obvious from further study that if the spray was allowed to reconcentrate the fire depressant had been washed away and fire risk became very high.

Two further groups arose in the class, one noting the different ways in which various sprays affected the growth of plants, studied wild flowers to discover which were most likely to be killed by which sprays and at which times of the year controlling sprays could be used without damage to more attractive vegetation, e.g. primroses. Another group

Approaches to language teaching

studied the eating habits of British birds in order to find which species might be most affected by noxious sprays.

When collated all the material was represented on charts and in book form and groups of children from the lower classes were taken on a tour of the materials, the fourth year children explaining the information more fully. Finally the class designed a resource unit to store relevant material which would be helpful to a group of children from the third year who had decided to continue the study by looking at the effects of sprays on the water supply and freshwater fish.

The project took up two to three hours per week for nearly two terms but the effects upon thinking and the range of skill development was immense. The children became adept at extracting information required from larger documents and by comparative reading began to detect bias. They gained experience of the special forms of language in science and in legal documents as well as in text and reference books. They learned equally to adjust their reading strategy to skim for a general impression, scan for specific pieces of information and read intensively for detailed knowledge. Finally, they gained considerable experience in using reference skills and creating a resource system and index.

Example Seven *Football Transfer*
A small group of slow learning boys aged fourteen were overheard discussing reports of the proposed transfer of the footballer Gary Birtles from Nottingham Forest to Manchester United. Obviously the boys lacked clear, detailed information and were talking largely on the basis of brief television bulletins and hearsay evidence. It was suggested that all the reports on the matter from the daily newspapers should be collected and fuller information discovered.

The initial response was mixed. The boys were enthusiastic enough about the topic – it seemed more fun than many things they were asked to do in school. But they soon realized that the reading demand of newspapers was rather high for them. Their reading level was in the range of that of the average ten-to eleven-year-old child and sports reports in newspapers have a difficulty level ranging from about twelve-year to sixteen-year levels.

However, their first experience of being allowed to read cooperatively rather than in isolation was sufficient to demonstrate to them that they could read newspapers when they pooled all their resources of vocabulary, syntax and knowledge. They then willingly attacked the task.

They decided to collect what they felt to be facts from one report first, listed them and then compared other reports to see if there were any discrepancies or additional information. They realized quickly that some reporters had either failed to gather all the relevant information or had chosen not to present it all. Equally they noted that different conclusions were drawn by the various reporters usually concerning the apportioning of blame and a seeming endeavour to make someone feel a rogue.

The conclusions were discussed and the papers checked for evidence to support them. They saw that often statements were made without, or with very little supportive evidence. The boys checked back again and began to notice the differences in the form of language and vocabulary used. One paper referred to Birtles as 'slightly injured', another as 'badly injured'. One wrote of Manchester United as a 'fabulously rich club', another merely commented that they 'could afford such a large fee'. They then checked crucial words and phrases across the accounts and were able to find that the conclusion drawn by the reporter was usually signalled by his choice of language and by the selection of the information reported.

During the reading, collation, representation and discussions, the boys learned a great deal about the means of detecting bias and prejudice in text, the intentions of newspapers and the reading strategies needed to use them wisely. In addition the cooperation among them aided their language and reading development and the successful experience gave them a greater measure of motivation to improve their reading skill further.

Some conclusions

The above examples represent but a tiny sample of the possibilities for the integrated teaching of the language arts across the whole curriculum. However, they do demonstrate several features which are central to the effective design of a language curriculum:

- activities must cover a wide range of purposes, varied media and situations.

- the special forms of language for personal, imaginative and informational processing must be given an appropriate balance and the thinking and language specific to certain subject areas must be introduced.

- in written language the children must receive opportunities and instruction across a much wider front than the traditional concentration on matters of word identification, spelling and comprehension. These include purpose setting, planning, selecting desired outcomes, media selection, indexing, resource skills etc. None of these can be dealt with adequately by structured teaching materials but demand that the child is placed in problem solving and discovery situations to complete realistic tasks.

3

Diagnostic teaching

Diagnosis as a term is not very popular with teachers. It seems to conjure up visions of batteries of formal frightening tests given in one-off interviews by psychologists which appear to have little direct effect upon the learning and teaching situation. The problems associated with the use of standardized and criterion-referenced test materials have already been discussed (see pp. 64–67) and a plea made for the use of informal observation techniques. For all that, the term *diagnosis* remains the best description of the activity, for it simply means finding out. If teaching is to be appropriate for each individual child we must be able to describe the stage of development reached and the type of performance being made. The process of *diagnosis* is not one which merely aims to find out a child's difficulties or weaknesses. Instead it seeks to understand more fully the total language processing of the child so that a sound assessment can be made of his needs and thereby his likely success at a higher level. The observations should also reveal the information needed to decide on the type of teaching strategy and methods which might best achieve the fulfilment of such needs.

Diagnostic teaching refers to the constant observation of children in learning situations from which the teacher frames hypotheses, ideas about the needs of the child, which are then tested out in new learning situations. These are in turn observed and whenever necessary new hypotheses and more new learning situations and strategies are devised. As such, diagnostic teaching is a circular process which continues throughout school life. It can be represented diagrammatically as follows:

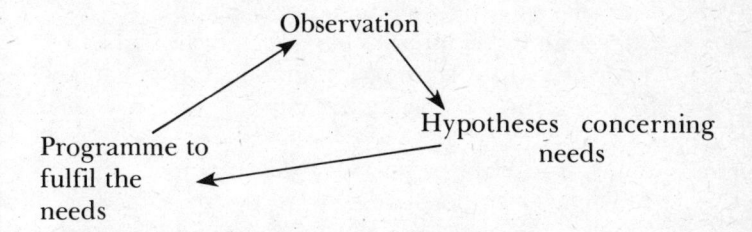

```
            Observation
           ↗          ↘
Programme to          Hypotheses concerning
fulfil the   ←──────      needs
needs
```

As has been mentioned earlier, informal observations do bring problems and these can only be overcome by acknowledging their existence and nature; through extensive practice and the increasing sophistication of techniques for the collation and analysis of the observations. The major problems are:

1 Subjectivity – it is all too easy to interpret observations in such a way as to make them fit an expected result. In miscue analysis, for example, the teacher who gives a heavy weighting in her teaching programme to phonic work is likely to view miscues in largely phonic terms and ignore clues which suggest grammatical or meaning problems may be causes of errors.

2 The difficulty of observing from the child's language behaviour in everyday situations any problems which arise from a weakness in a subskill area. For example, a child might show obvious weaknesses in comprehension but the child's difficulty could lie in areas such as a lack of background knowledge, a low level of conceptual development, insufficient knowledge of vocabulary, lack of understanding of certain syntactical structures, inability to observe sequences or cause and effect relationships, lack of ability to process the style of the

speaker or author, inability to maintain a clear purpose to guide the task, etc.

3 There is often a tendency to jump to conclusions from too small an amount of evidence. Observations need to be made in a variety of situations, using different techniques and the information collated and carefully analysed before learning programmes are changed. Since it is rare for a single error to suggest that a child has a particular need observations have to be continued until clear patterns of behaviour are compiled. This may seem long-winded but the time spent will usually make teaching and learning more economic and equally prevent us giving children tasks which may be too difficult or inappropriate and thus develop feelings of failure or boredom.

4 Hypotheses can be set in too narrow a frame in the rush of the decision making in a busy classroom. It is important, therefore, that the teacher establishes clear aims and objectives in relation to her expectancy of what the children are to attain within a given period. Equally the teacher must have a knowledge of the diversity of learning routes by which children can proceed from one stage of development to another, depending upon their abilities and preferred styles of learning.

5 When a diagnostic teaching procedure is established the traps are to overemphasize the difficulties of the child rather than ensuring his overall success and to teach isolated subskills rather than including their usage in holistic and realistic learning situations. This demand that all skill learning be sited in tasks which fulfil the child's conscious needs and are valid for the experiences and knowledge gained is difficult to fulfil, but when achieved is far more rewarding for both child and teacher.

Suggested objectives of the language learning programme

The overall aim suggested in chapter 1 of this book is that children will develop into independent learners and thinkers. Language learning plays a crucial role in achieving this aim. The most profitable route to success will be through the integrated teaching of the language arts across the curriculum. However, for convenience of listing the objectives to be achieved are broken down into divisions of the ways in which language is used.

Objectives

Over the period of school life the children should master the following understandings and uses of language and it should be noted that work towards these objectives can in the majority of cases begin from the commencement of school life.

Oral language

- an understanding of the nature and function of language as a symbolic representation of meaning whether considered personally or shared with others
- the enlargement of vocabulary
- the understanding of word meanings and the variance of meaning occasioned by the context in which the word is set
- the understanding of the grammatical functions of words and modifications to word forms which are grammatically imposed, e.g. run, ran, running
- the ability to predict the likelihood of parts of speech occurring in an incomplete flow of language

- the ability to predict meaning and the likely occurrence of certain words from an incomplete flow of language
- to understand and use grammatical forms appropriate to particular situations, e.g. the use of the passive voice in reporting scientific experiments
- the understanding and use of intonation, pause and emphasis and the impact of variation of these upon meaning
- to understand and use language appropriate to specific situations such as questions, directions, reports, the presentation of information and the pursuit of an argument
- the ability to retell and create stories
- the ability to understand and create art forms of language in poetry and drama
- the understanding and use of language in interpersonal and social relationships
- the thoughtful appraisal and use of language
- achieve tolerance of, and ability to process dialectical language forms
- to enjoy, use freely and develop good attitudes towards spoken language

Written language

1 Reading

(a) Attitudes and understandings

- the understanding and use of the language we use to talk about language (metalanguage)

Diagnostic teaching

- the appreciation of the forms and purposes of written communication
- the form and constraints of written language, e.g. left-right orientation and punctuation
- the differences between written and spoken forms of language
- that reading is concerned with the thoughtful consideration of meaning to fulfil a purpose
- the appreciation of reading and writing as enjoyable and meaningful pursuits

(b) Word identification

- understanding of the nature of words and word boundaries
- the understanding and use of words as having meaning and that precise meanings are constrained by the context in which they occur
- the immediate recognition of words by their shape and composition
- the techniques of associating sounds of speech with the symbols of which the written word is composed
- the use of spoken language and background subject knowledge to predict the function and meaning of a word within a context
- the ability to use a strategy of combining all aspects of word attack to approach an unknown word.

(c) Comprehension and study

- the marshalling of background knowledge of language and subject matter for the thoughtful processing of an author's meaning

- the processing of meaning at different levels according to the purpose for reading, e.g. skimming for a general impression of the story line in reading a novel for pleasure

- the recognition and ordering of an author's main and subordinate ideas

- the appreciation of cause and effect relationships

- the making of critical judgements and decisions

- the selection and collation of information which the reader wishes to retain

- the processing of a wide variety of forms in which information may be economically and clearly represented, e.g. precis, diagrammatical devices, etc.

(d) Planning

- the techniques of consideration of purpose and the setting of desired outcomes to achieve them

- the ability to use reference systems and surveying techniques to select materials of the appropriate type, content and level to suit a purpose

- to recognize author purpose and different writing styles and modify reading behaviour accordingly, e.g. to be able to recognize and compensate for author bias.

2 Writing

- gain an understanding of the purposes of written communication

- the development of an economic and legible writing style

- the ability to modify the form of writing according to

the type and purpose of the material being created

- the understanding of the function of word boundaries, sentence constructions and punctuation
- the selection of appropriate vocabulary and ability to conform to grammatical rules, e.g. the use of inflectional endings of words
- an understanding of the necessity of standard spelling within written communication
- the establishment of learning techniques to master the spelling of new words
- the understanding of the purposes and uses of a thesaurus and dictionary

Observational situations and techniques

1 Appreciation and use of oral language

In surveying the spoken language usage of children and their ability to respond appropriately to the language of others, there are two major areas which demand consideration.

(a) The child's understanding and use of the range of language functions. Some classification frameworks for language functions appear later in this section. Function here refers to the purpose for which the language was used, e.g. to communicate a personal need or to request information.

(b) The range of the child's vocabulary and usage of grammar.

Both these areas will be influenced by the nature of the communication task as well as by the level and type of development of the child. For example, in retelling a story the child may omit to use such functions as reasoning or hypothesizing or restrict his use of tenses and yet quite successfully achieve the objective set. Firstly, therefore, the child's performance must be judged in terms of the nature of the task set and secondly, the teacher must ensure that observations are taken across a range of tasks in order to compile a realistic picture of the child's language development.

A considerable knowledge can be accrued by eavesdropping on the informal conversations of small groups of children – though this can be a very lengthy procedure and result in a far from balanced view of each child's development. More profitable would be the setting up of various types of situations in relation to the ongoing work of the classroom. In this way the various functions of language can be covered and a check made as to whether the child recognizes which functions are appropriate to which situation. This approach should equally prove to be more economic of time for the teacher.

The transcripts that follow are examples of some of the variety of language tasks which can be formulated to check particular aspects. After studying them and the classifications of language functions which have been used in their analysis, the reader will no doubt be able to think up many others which would fit happily into the everyday situation and curriculum of the classroom, so becoming an integral part of the work rather than appearing as a test situation.

Diagnostic teaching

Example One *Building with Lego*
(Dean, a five-year-old boy, in a school setting, is set the task of building a house from Lego bricks and the teacher stimulates him by questions to verbalize his planning and describe his actions.)

T	I want you to build a house for me with lego.
T	Will your house have windows?
Dean	/I'm going to put the² windows in there/ ... /No, I⁴ can't cos nobody can see/ ... /I know, cos the⁴ table is there./
T	Will your house have a door?
Dean	/Here's the³ chimney./ /I can't undo³ these bricks./ /I've got to find³ a door./
T	What colour bricks are you going to use to build your box?
Dean	/Bricks / ... /We've got ³all different colours/
T	Who lives in your house?
Dean	In our house³ – me dad/
T	When you've built your house what kind of furniture will you put inside?
Dean	/Furniture³/ ... /You don't need guns in⁴ houses but one on the wall one on the wall./
T	What else will you have inside your house?
Dean	/Sometimes toys, but we³ 'aven't got no toys in 'ere/ 'ave¹ we?
T	No, we haven't
T	How is Santa Claus going to get in?
Dean	/No can't³ fit in it/

97

Children's Words

> T   Can't he?
>
> Dean   /No³/
>
> T   What are you going to put in your garden?
>
> Dean   Er³ . . . /we 'aven't got no³ toys/ and we 'aven't got a tortoise in there/² . . . /I'll use that² for the windows/ . . . /You don't need a gun on . . .² on the . . . er . . . House . . ./ top /of the³ house./ /No dad, throw'd³ our bed out/ . . . /so we got our baby's bed/. So /our³ baby s. .s. .sleeps in³ our Marie's bed . . . bed . . . bed./
>
> T   Your Dad, what did you say?
>
> Dean   /Me dad throw'd³ the bed/ . . . /our bed³ out. So we got a front room and our baby³ sleeps in our . . . our Marie's bed/ . . . /so my Dad . . . /so we got three beds/ . . . /but we sleepin³ a bed . . . a baby's bed,/ and /me mum sleeps in³ the back bed/ . . . /There's another window like that one/³ . . . /putting the windows² here/. /Do you know where² the teacher gone?/
>
> T   She's sick.
>
> Dean   Yea.⁷ She is . . ./He said, 'Sweet Head³'. a head is a sweet./

Classifications

There are many classifications of the functions or uses of language. Two such classifications are used here, the first based on the work of Tough, the second on Halliday. The numbers placed over the text of the transcript refer to the Tough analysis. The units of utterances, i.e. the smallest meaningful units of speech are shown by oblique lines.

Diagnostic teaching

Tough analysis categories

1 *Self-maintaining*: utterances which refer to individual needs or interests, justify behaviour, criticize or threaten others.

2 *Directing*: utterances which monitor actions or direct actions of self or others.

3 *Reporting*: statements concerning past or present experiences.

4 *Reasoning*: explanation of processes, the recognition of relationships, justification of actions, reflection upon events and the recognition of principles.

5 *Predicting*: anticipation of events, problems and their solutions and the prediction of outcomes.

6 *Projecting*: projecting speech to enter into the experiences and feelings of others or the anticipation of situations not previously experienced.

7 *Imagining*: developing imaginary situations or stories.

Table 1 Dean (Tough model)

	Classification	Score
1	Self maintaining	2
2	Directing	5
3	Reporting	20
4	Reasoning	3
5	Predicting	–
6	Projecting	–
7	Imagining	1

Halliday analysis categories

1 *Instrumental*: means of getting things done, e.g. 'I want ...', 'I need ...'

2 *Regulatory*: to regulate the behaviour of self and others – rules and instructions.

3 *Interactional*: social interaction, getting along with others.

4 *Personal*: shaping of the self through interaction with others. Expression of personal feelings and attitudes.

5 *Heuristic*: explanation of the environment, investigation and questioning.

6 *Imaginative*: language used to create an environment – 'Let's pretend . . .'

7 *Representational*: transmission of subject matter and ideas.

Table 2 Dean (Hallidays model)

	INSTRUMENTAL	REGULATORY	INTERACTIONAL	PERSONAL	HEURISTIC	IMAGINATIVE	REPRESENTATIONAL
Question 1			√		√		
2			√				
3			√				
4			√				
5			√				
6			√	√			
7			√		√		
8			√	√			

Diagnostic teaching

Commentary

First impressions would suggest that the teacher's leads could have been much more extended and thus have led Dean to express far more language of the reasoning and projecting types which are almost entirely absent in this transcript. However, by the intonation in his responses to the teacher's questions, or indeed complete silence whilst he carried on with his building task, Dean often made it quite clear that further exploration of that topic was of no interest to him. This was particularly clear in relation to the references to Santa Claus, which seemed quite reasonable as the encounter took place in early December.

Significantly the only lengthy stretches of language are largely related to past experiences which the task in hand recalls to Dean. Whereas in his single sentence answers to questions, his use of sentence structure is quite good, this is not true of the longer flows of speech. It almost appears as though he is talking to himself rather than to the teacher, which explains the lack of necessity for the formality of sentence construction.

It is to be expected that the majority of utterances here would be of the reporting type, for after all Dean is largely describing what he is doing. However, many children with such a task at this stage would have vocalized rather more concerning the way they were directing their actions and given more evidence of their thinking and planning by statements under the headings of reasoning, predicting and projecting. In fact the transcript does reflect well the general state of the child, i.e. a rather low attention span, a tendency to allow his thoughts to wander and to be over-restricted to the concrete situation, thus using trial and error approaches to the task rather than a thoughtful prediction of possible solutions.

Dean undoubtedly needs more of these concrete type situations. But in order to develop his language and thinking, the teacher must stimulate him with questions of the type 'Now how do you think we can do that?' Another approach to the problem would be to set up situations where two or more children have to interact to find solutions such as are recorded in the following transcripts. Often in the individual situation the child does little more than answer direct questions, whereas in the group setting alongside his peers he is more likely to be uninhibited and argue in more detail for his point of view. Observing such situations the teacher can obtain a more detailed idea of the child's thinking and language development.

Even in this short transcript Dean reveals a number of grammatical errors which are fairly common at the five-year-old level, for example the double negative, e.g. 'we haven't got no toys', incorrect verb forms, e.g. 'throwd', the omission of subject and verb auxiliary, e.g. '. . . putting the windows here'. At such an early stage the child is likely to be inhibited if the correct form is insisted on at all times. Indeed, some children may feel that their language is considered unsuitable for use in school and, not knowing the more acceptable forms, may refuse to risk failure by expressing themselves. The first step forward here will be the example of the teacher's speech and the correction of the child's speech, where absolutely necessary, is introduced gradually over a period of time.

Diagnostic teaching

Example Two *Making and seeing*

The two transcripts here are based upon the work of two nine-year-old boys who are set tasks, but on this occasion the teacher simply records their discussions and allows the task and the children to control the direction of their deliberations. In this type of situation the children are more likely to reveal the type and level of their thinking and language abilities than when there is questioning by the teacher. Similar observations can be made to those in Dean's transcript, namely of vocabulary, grammar, the range and quality of the uses of language employed. The most important part of the observation here is to assess whether the children are using language which is appropriate to the task.

A more detailed analysis framework has been used to examine the two discussions undertaken by the two boys, Brian and Peter, and the numbers inserted above each utterance refer to the following uses of language:

1 Questions
2 Comparisons
3 Opinions, e.g. I think, I shall, I want, I know
4 Tentativeness, e.g. could, should, shall, might, isn't it
5 Hesitations
6 Thinking pauses
7 Reasoning, e.g. because, if so that, like, wonder
8 Imagination
9 Reporting
10 Repetition

Transcript One: Origami

Here the children were given sheets of paper and written instructions on the construction of a paper boat and asked to help each other to complete the finished article. In addition to the general language features which can be observed, the specific vocabulary and concepts related to the task and the ability to understand instructions can also be assessed. We

Children's Words

will particularly be looking at the children's ability to hypothesize and give reasons for their actions.

B	/You have to read⁹ the instructions/ Both reading instructions /Fold a square⁹ of paper/
B	/Diagonal⁹/
Both	/Both ways,⁹ undo/
B	/Unfold/
P	/Undo, it doesn³'t say unfold/ /Fold the square⁹ of paper diagonal both ways/
B	/Undo⁹/
P	/Now No. 2 Fold straight⁹ across in half both ways undo/
P	/Here Brian look⁹ what I'm doing/
B	/Fold straight across⁹/
P	/We don³'t/we don¹⁰'t/
B	/Read that⁹ first/ /Fold the square of paper diagonally both ways/ Undo
P	/Fold straight⁹ across/Fold straight¹⁰ across/like² that/
B	/Across like that⁴ and then go like that// wouldn't it?/
P	/I think³ I can/
B	/Now fold it that⁹ way, put it like that then put it like that/
P	/You can't put it⁴ like/that can⁷ you?/ /Oh yes you can³ Brian/

104

B	/Oh no you³ can't/Come on let'⁴s just watch/ Fold it straight⁷ there like it said, like a triangle/ It must go like⁷ that/
P	/Fold along all the ⁹dotty lines in Fig 50/ Both Figure⁹ 50
B	/Undo after ⁹each fold/
P	/I've done⁹ that one Bri/
B	/Now I get³ it/
B	/It goes like⁹ that Peter/ Look
P	/I think I've got³ the idea Brian, fold it like that/
B	/You³ don't/
P	/You³ do/ – fold it into a square⁹ first. I mean an oblong/ Look Brian look
B	/You do it like⁹ that, then you do it like that/
B	You can't/
P	/You can³/
B	/You³ don't/
P	/You do/
P	/Alright, fold⁹ it like that/
B	/There's something³ wrong/
P	/Fold it like⁹ that/
B	/Fold it like⁹ that and then you . . ./
P	. . ./on the ⁹other side, look/
B	/Like that then⁹ like that/
P	/Now how do you¹ do that?/
B	/Peter come here⁹ a minute/

Children's Words

P	/I'll show y̖ou/I've done tha̋t one too big/
B	... /and over like̖ that there/ ... /the̖ sails/ /You need that part a̖nd the part for the sail/
P	/And then you do̖ that/
B	/I think you've gőt it wrong Peter/
P	/I think that yőu put your hand in there and (tape not clear)/
B	/That's the same look̗ its gorra need the sail/
B	/It's only got one sőide of it/
P	/We've got that pa̋rt right/
B	/Yea we have, all thé rest are harder/
B	/We have to do̖ a/ /Come on – how do ẙou do the sails?/ /you thought I thought̋ that we got it wrong/
P	/– this part i̋sn't wrong though/ /This part i̋s right/
B	/Now you fold it/
P	/Yea that's̋ right – /not there,̋ that way/ /That's̋ it/
B	/And the othe̖r way you do don't you?/
P	/Open it̖ up/
B	/And do the othe̖r way like that/
P	/And now you go̖ like that/ /And now you go̖ like this/
B	/Now you go̖/
B	/You don't̋ go like that/
P	/Yőu do/

106

Diagnostic teaching

B /You don't³ go like that/

P /You go like³ that and then this way/

B /I'll do the crease⁹ and now you go like this/

B /Peter, I've done⁹ it wrong/

P /It won't be, your⁹ right there your right/

B /That's it … the² little/ – there

P /That's³ right/

B /What¹/

P /That part's³ right. I think you fold³ it up like that Bri/

B /Do you¹?/

P /Yes³/

B /You're right³/
/Now how do¹ you do them?/that's not right⁷ because/
/I didn't know⁹ how to do it/

P /We'd best think⁷ a bit first Bri/

B /Yea we should, think¹⁰, think think/ – /that's what we've got to think¹⁰/ With our own¹⁰ brains right/

P Of course we'll have to⁷ help each other/

B /We've done half of it right⁹. You don't do that, you don't put it over like a square/ – like a rectangle² now/

P /Where's the instructions¹ Bri?/

B /Not like³ that/

P /It's right³,/there's the instructions⁹/

107

Children's Words

B	/I've got it right,³/there's the line the cross and circle/⁹ /Sh, I've got to³ think – come on think/
P	/We've got that³ part right/
B	/Yea we don't know³ what else to do/
P	/Hey Brian where's¹ the sail?/
B	/We've got it right⁴ haven't we?/look⁹/
P	/We've got that⁴ part right/
B	/Gor⁹ it/
P	/One, two, three, four,⁹ five, six, seven/
B	/You don't know³ what to do do ya?/
P	/It's like³ that/
B	/It's not³/
P	/It is,³/you⁹ look/
B	/It's like³ that/
B	/Come⁹ on/
P	/It's like³ that/
B	/No it's³ not/
P	/Yea it³ is/
B	/Yea it's like that/
P	/Come⁹ on/
B	/I've got it³ I think/I've got the hang⁴ of it now/
P	/You do go like³ that Brian/I told ya⁹ ya did/ /It's a³ rocket/
B	/Just show me how¹ you do it/come on⁹ Peter
P	/Yea Brian,⁹ /Gerr of it Brian/ or I'll tell you purit like² that/ and /bring it round like⁹ that

108

Diagnostic teaching

B	/Now what élse?¹/
P	/Fig 52 bóat⁹/. Fig 52 bòat¹⁰/
P	/That is what oúr³ boats, boats called/
P	/Now we've got this pàrt⁴ right haven't we?/
B	/We hàve³/
B	/I know wè³ have/
P	/Why don't¹ you, /it might stick pàrt⁴ like that Bri/
B	/It might stìck² like that/
P	/Get from under⁹ there – that boat/
B	/Yours is bìgger² than mine/ I wonder⁷ why?/
P	/Ah, I knòw³ it now/
P	/Ah ha oh ho Brian stop⁹ messing/ /Don't mess⁹ Brian/
B	/Don't mess⁹ Peter/
P	/Don't do that⁹ again/
B	/Don't do that⁹ again/
B	Peter
B	Brian
B	/Don't do that⁹ Peter/
P	/OK now come⁹ on Brian/
B	/Come⁹ on – /what are you doing¹ yourself now?/
P	/I knòw³ it now/
B	/What you dò³ – that's it/
P	/Rubbish, rùbbish³/
B	/It is it's³ a triangle/

109

P	/I know but what about the sails?¹/
B	/Will you show¹ me now/
P	/Where's the sails?¹/
P	/Where is the¹ sails gone?/
P	/Now like⁹ that/ Now Brian you have⁹ to think, now – think/
B	/Think, think,¹⁰ think/
P	Singing
B	/Come on, stop⁹ messing Peter
P	/You stop messing⁹ Brian/
B	/now before the boat⁷ is finished
P	/Put em⁹ back again/
B	/Now think, think, think,¹⁰ think, think/
P	/Think,¹⁰ think – gerroff Brian. /I'll tell I'll tell¹⁰ now. /Tell Brian to stop⁹ messing/
B	/Come⁹ on,/come on¹⁰/
B	/Well stop messing⁹ Peter/
P	/Stop messing⁹ Brian/
B	/Come⁹ on/ is that the¹ way Peter?/
P	(Singing) /Robin Hood, Robin Hood,⁸ riding through the . . ./
B	/Stop it⁹ Peter/
P	/Fold⁹ P,/fold¹⁰ P/
B	/We've done⁹ that one/
P	/No we haven't³/
B	/We have³/

P	Brian use E F G H a̍s⁹ your base and bring J K L and M/
B	/J̍ekl⁹/ J̍ekl¹⁰/
P	/Toge̍ther⁹/
B	/The four corner⁹ will then stand/ ex e̍x¹⁰/
P	/E̍xit⁷/Exit that's it/ (knock on door)
P	/Where we̍re¹ we up to,/you go like̍³ that Brian/
P	/O P Q E F – now⁹ this one then/
B	/P was u̍pwards⁷/
P	/I've got it³, Brian/ Lo̍ok⁹/
B	/It will end⁷ up wrong/
P	/We wo̍n't³/ /Only follow the instructions⁷ then you'll get it/ right/
B	/Pe̍ter¹/
P	/Wha̍t¹/
B	/Will you¹ just do that for me/
B	/Pe̍ter¹/
P	/Wha̍t¹/
B	/Do you do it like that a̍nd⁴ like that that and that/
P	/Oh B̍ri³/
B	/Pe̍ter¹/
P	/You go like³ that. /I'll do it⁹ for ya/
B	/You go like⁴ that don't you/
P	/See, I told³ ya/

Children's Words

B /I've got $\overset{3}{\text{that}}$ wrong/

P /You have $\overset{3}{\text{got}}$ it wrong 'aven't ya?/

P $\overset{1}{\text{Brian}}$

B Mumbles instructions

P /$\overset{1}{\text{Brian}}$/

B /Y$\overset{9}{\text{e}}$s/

P /I've done $\overset{9}{\text{that}}$ one there/ Fold figure backwards along dotted $\overset{1}{\text{line}}$ AB where's AB/
/Ah we $\overset{3}{\text{right}}$/
/Were's $\overset{1}{\text{mine}}$/

B /Here$\overset{9}{\text{'s}}$ yours/

P $\overset{9}{\text{Brian}}$

B /You go $\overset{4}{\text{like}}$ that?/

P /N$\overset{3}{\text{o}}$/

B /You go $\overset{4}{\text{like}}$ that?/

P /N$\overset{3}{\text{o}}$/

B /So you've $\overset{7}{\text{only}}$ got O there/'aven't $\overset{4}{\text{ya}}$?/
/I've only $\overset{7}{\text{got}}$ to push em back/

P /You've only $\overset{9}{\text{got}}$ O there/ and you've $\overset{2}{\text{got}}$ one triangle

P /And one $\overset{3}{\text{square}}$/

B /That isn$\overset{3}{\text{'t}}$ a square, /only that$\overset{2}{\text{'s}}$ a square/ is that $\overset{1}{\text{the}}$ one?

P /Now this is your $\overset{1}{\text{bit}}$ isn't it Bri/

B /Y$\overset{9}{\text{e}}$s/

P /I think I$\overset{3}{\text{'ve}}$ got it/

B /I think you$\overset{3}{\text{'ve}}$ got it yea/
Mumbling instructions

Diagnostic teaching

	/If only you could get[7] it up the side and fold it over you would have it/
P	/This is the[3] hard bit/
B	/I think I've got it[3] Peter/ /You got that and[7] you can get it over there/
P	/Yes[9]/
B	/then fold it over[7] you will have it/
P	/I will have[9] it/
B	/Yes[9] you[3] will./ Don't do that[7] though/Don't mess Peter/
P	/I think that's the way isn't it[4]/
B	/nearly[9]/ nearly[10]/ done[9] it/
P	/Bri that's it[3]/
B	/Pull that corner[9] out that's it/ /Pull that corner out and[9] you will have it/
B	/Yea/
P	/That isn't it[3]/
B	/Bend right[9]/ – I've got[3] it Peter/
P	/Let's see[9] – yes/ Long pause[6]
P	/Nearly done[9] it Brian/
B	/That one[9]/ – that's the other[2]/ set charging[8] to attack/
P	That's[2] yours
P	/We may have 2 each[4] we don't know yet, do we? /And that one is[9] misses/ (pointing to the 5 boats)
B	/Put mine there[9]/

113

Children's Words

Table 3 Peter and Brian (Origami analysis)

		1	2	3	4	5	6	7	8	9	10
Peter		14	6	48	5	–	1	5	1	44	7
	%	10.7	4.6	36.7	3.8	–	.8	3.8	.8	33.6	5.3
Brian		14	6	42	10	–	–	14	–	46	7
	%	10	4.3	30.2	7.2	–	–	10	–	33.1	5

Peter: total utterances 131
Brian: total utterances 139

Transcript Two: Watching the bird
Here the same two boys, Brian and Peter, are observed watching a budgerigar in a cage, describing what they see. We shall be able to observe their powers of description but would also hope that they will hypothesize the reason about the behaviour of the bird.

B	/He's playing with his⁹ bells/ isn't⁴ he?/Er now⁵ he's rubbing his feet,⁹ now he's looking/
Both	/In the mirror⁹/
B	/He's sitting⁹ on his/
P	/Not/
Both	/He's sitting on⁹ the end of his ladder/
B	/He's playing with his⁹ bells again/
P	/He isn't, see⁹ see/ (not clear) . . . /end of the ladder/
B	/He's playing with his bell still, he's playing with his bell again, now/
P	/Er he's⁵ . . ./
Both	/He's on his⁹ perch/

114

Diagnostic teaching

B	/He's swinging the mir̊ror er and the bell/
Both	/And he's p̊ecking the bell/
B	/and he's m̊oving about and he's moving his beak and this she, – and his feathers sticking off the end and getting on to the bars, he's moving his head . . ./
P	/Around, er̊ squeaking/
B	/Yeah, he's̊ whistling/
P	/Er you could call it squeaking, yeah/
B	/And you could call it . . ./
P	/The other thing/
B	/whistling/
P	/Now he's̊ jumping/
B	/Flew on̊ to the bars/
P	/and he̊ jumped/
B	/And noẘ he's playing with his, with his water/
P	/Drinking̊ it too/
B	/Drinking̊ it yes, pulling off/
P	/His the s̊ide and pecking in his water/
B	/And he's p̊ecking the plastic off the water/
P	/Pecking the pl̊astic water/
B	/Now his head has̊ gone a little bit backwards, /now he's annoyed /and he's whistling, now hè is shouting at us/ 'cos we're talking/
P	(giggles) /and now h̊e she's . . ./
B	/And looking at us̊ with his one eye/
P	/Long John Silver/

Children's Words

B   /Yea/

B   /Yeah^{10}/

P   /Joey, Joey, Joey, and Joey,^{5} Joey, Joey, er . . ./

B   /He's been eating his^9 seed now he's on the ground pecking on his Teddy Bear now he's . . ./

P   /hugging^6 him/

B   /Now he's playing^9 with his bell and then and there's all feathers on the/

P   /ground/ (giggle)

B   /Now he's now^{10} he's/ gone up the ladder^9 playing with his bell again (giggles) and now he's back on his perch again, and he's down the ladder back on his^9 teddy again/

P   /Pecking his^9 teddy bear/

B   /And he went^{10} and he went/ down the ladder^9 and the bell began to ring and then^{10}/ and then/ and the wheels^9 (tape not clear)

P   /Once upon^8 a time/

B   Now /now^{10}/ he's just looking^9 at the cage . . ./

P   /And pecking in^9 his eye . . ./

B   / . . .^{5}/the /teddy bears eye^9 and he's pecking on his nose and he's going up and the bells starting to ring, ringing and going up the ladder er he's stopped now/

P   /He's stopped^9/

B   /And he's^9 back on his perch again/

P   /And he rang^9 his bell/

B   /And he's^9/

116

Diagnostic teaching

P /And scratching his feathers/

B /And cleaning his feathers/

P /And scratching them/

B /Yeah, and he's looking at us, he's on his teddy bear again/

P /Peck, peck pecking teddy bear's eye/

B /And his tails fell out, it's back in again, and he's back on the other perch/ and now he's annoyed again/ now he's playing with the seed/

P /And er/ he's walking about on his perch and screeching/

B /Yeah/ (giggle) /and er and/ his feathers are in the ladder and now he's whistling again/

P /Now he's drinking his water and/

B /Eating seeds/

P /And look/ and /look that that/ that that that/sandpaper down there, yeah and now the .../

B /The bottom bell's ringing and there's blue feathers/and there's blue feathers/ on the bottom of the sandpaper now he's going down on the bars and he's just jumped on the bars he's going down now, he's /on the the/

Both /his ladder/

P /Again/

B /And he's playing with his teddy bear rocking him/

P (Singing) /rock a bye baby on the tree top,/ and and what is he doing?/

Children's Words

B /He's lo̊oking at . . ./

P /Out of h̊is cage/

B /Now he's annŏtated/ now his beak's mo̊ving and he's and his/ tongue/

P /Don't pull tongues at/ us er/ and and . . ./

B /He's he's/ annoyed/ and now his beak — he's hanging onto the bars/

P /And he's spilling his water/

B /Yes/

P /Now he's playing with his water now again/

B /He's playing with the iron, with the cross/

P /And yeah, playing with the iron bars/

B /And he was scratching/ scratching/ himself on the bars and now he's looking in his water/

P /Now he's mad again/

B /Now he's er,/ now/ he's mad again/

P /Now he's looking at Brian/

B /Now he's looking at Peter./ /and and/ now he's looking at his water./

P /Yeah/ through the through/ the plastic glass

B /And now he's mad/

P /And his water spilled and his seed is off/

P /And his screeching/

B /And he's . . ./ he is pushing his chest out./

P /And now he's with/ . . . not clear . . .

B (Brian imitates whistle) /that's what he went like/

118

Diagnostic teaching

B /And he's been drínking his water and eating the seeds/ and the and the/ ladders moved because he knocked it/ and the bells rínging again.

P /And the líttle bell too/

B /And he's loóking in his mirror again/

P /And what elsé is he doing?'

B /And he's loóking at the steel and he's just going and he just went/ (giggles) /And er what's he doing now?/

P /Screeching again/

B /Now he's scréeching again/

P /I wonder whát/ he is scréeching for?/

B /I don't know/ and he's whístling/

P /scréeching again/

B /Yea now he's whístling again/

P /And his chest cóming out/

B /And his back féathers is out of the cage/ Now and he's now/ he's playing with his steel/

P /or métal /or íron/

B /And and and/now he's jumped on the swíng and looking in the mirror again and on his perch and he keep on and he's pecking at his window/

Both And iròn glass/the mírror

B /And his feathers stícking out again/

P /Miss cóming/

B /And now he's whístling again and his feathers on the ladder/

119

P /And now he's walk$\overset{9}{\text{i}}$ng backwards off the other perch/ Now he's annoy$\overset{3}{\text{e}}$d again/'cos we'$\overset{7}{\text{re}}$ talking/

B /And$\overset{10}{\text{ }}$ and/ he's annoy$\overset{3}{\text{e}}$d again/ he's look$\overset{9}{\text{i}}$ng through the bars at trays. He's messing in his mirror again. And he's just flapped his wings/ /And he wen$\overset{9}{\text{t}}$ up again/

P /He's doing a$\overset{9}{\text{ }}$lot of things, your not watching him/

B /Now he's looking$\overset{9}{\text{ }}$at us now again/

P /He's pecking$\overset{9}{\text{ }}$at his mirror/

Table 4 Peter and Brian (Watching the bird analysis)

		1	2	3	4	5	6	7	8	9	10
Peter		18	4	18	3	–	7	9	2	32	30
	%	14.6	3.3	14.6	2.4	–	5.7	7.3	1.6	26	24.4
Brian		19	1	20	–	–	3	24	5	17	10
	%	19.2	1.01	20.2	–	–	3	24.2	5.05	17.2	10.10

Peter : total utterances 123
Brian : total utterances 99

Commentary

It is interesting to note that the two boys play rather different roles in the two discussions. In the *Origami* discussion Brian is dominant and this appears to be related to his greater expertise in craft-type pursuits and perhaps his ability to read instructions with greater clarity. In *Watching the bird*, however, Peter is more frequently taking on the leadership role again perhaps pointing to the strengths exerted by interest or background knowledge.

The language types elicited by both tasks from the boys

varies rather more with the task than with the individual differences in the two boys. An earlier suggestion should be recalled here that it is necessary to erect a variety of tasks in order to have a full knowledge of the use of the variety of language functions by any individual child.

For example, in the *Origami* transcript there are frequent examples of comparisons and statements of opinion whereas in *Watching the bird* few examples of these uses of speech appeared. Likewise, there was more evidence of reasoning in the *Origami* discussion than in *Watching the bird* though the latter did evoke some statements which revealed imaginative thinking.

Repetition was a feature of both discussions but in different forms. Peter's repetitions were largely in the discussion on *Watching the bird* and tended to be repetitions of earlier descriptive comments whereas Brian's within the *Origami* task are related to impressing upon Peter his reasoning concerning the solutions to the problems arising from the interpretation of the instructions.

Watching the bird was a very restricted, narrow task and really needed the interaction of the teacher to extend the thinking and uses of language. The vocabulary of the children showed obvious limitations, e.g. 'iron bars' as a description of the cage and their inability to find words to describe the various sounds made by the bird. This particular discussion would have been expected to have produced a much wider vocabulary than was used by the two boys and it becomes obvious that the range of adjectives and adverbs particularly, within their vocabulary, is very limited.

In the *Origami* discussion there were far more interjections, disagreements and shorter, less complex sentences than in *Watching the bird*. This is probably related to the more mechanical nature of the task and to the language of instructions provided as a stimulus. In comparing the two transcripts, however, it is easy to see that the first would have given a false impression of the range of syntax which both children were capable of using.

Children's Words

The stimulation of these boys to develop a wider vocabulary, their use of syntax and the variety and appropriate usage of the various language functions would be helped by further discussions based in both concrete and abstract tasks but in a slightly larger group so that they may benefit from exposure to the language and thinking of other children. Most important, however, will be the interaction of the teacher to stimulate thinking and suggest wider vocabulary for their consideration. The hope here in general language terms would be to enlarge the usage of hypothesizing and reasoning which were not as evident in the transcripts as could have been hoped.

Diagnostic teaching

Example Three *Poison bottles*
It is interesting to note the differences which occur within and across groups when involved in the same type of task. In the following task two groups of children were given four identical bottles of liquid and asked to discuss how they could discover which one of the four was filled with poison. The two groups were selected from the same class of children, the first group was a group of poorer readers, the second of more fluent readers. A further more detailed framework for analysis has been used here and the numbers over the utterances in the two transcripts refer to the following classifications.

1. Maze
2. Reporting
3. Reasoning
4. Personal
5. Arguing
6. Collaborating
7. Recognizing a principle
8. Comparing
9. Justifying
10. Tentativeness
11. Hypothesizing
12. Questioning

Transcript One: Poison bottles
(Discussion among a group of non-fluent readers)

A	/I think it's that bottle[11] there/
J	/And I think it's that one because[11] it looks awful pale and it looks brown at the bottom/
M	/And I think it's that one because[11] that's brown at the bottom as well/
S	/And I think it's that one because[11] it looks very brown at the top/

123

Children's Words

Tchr   But can you tell me why you think it's poison?

A   /'Cos it's brown/ (it's brown, brown) at the bottom/

....

Tchr   Tea is brown – that's not poison is it?

A   No

....

J   /That one/

Tchr   Why?

J   /Well it looks pale 'cos you can't see through it properly/ and it looks a bit brown at the bottom (but) – /I think it looks funny (like) – /it looks like it's got things coming down/

Tchr   Margaret.

M   /It's brown but it's all white at t'top/

....

Tchr   Why would that make it poison?

M   /Cos there shouldn't be brown at bottom/

Tchr   Shouldn't be?

M   /No it should be white all t'way down/

....

Tchr   Do you think some poison is white all the way down?

A   /Yeh sometimes some are white all t'way through like water/ when there's a pipe leaking it goes brown and germs get in your water/

S   /Em – that one it looks/ like it looks/ white like you can see through it/ and it looks like a browness (at top) at the top/

....

124

Diagnostic teaching

Tchr	All right that's how it looks. Is there any other way you might tell it's poison besides looking at it?

....
....

J	/Colour¹⁰ of it/
A	/It looks darker² at bottom/
Tchr	We've thought about colour. Any other way?
S	/There's a black thing on top² of that one on top of t'water/¹² whatever it is/
J	/I can't see⁵ anything/
S	/That little black² thing there/
	Pause ....
Tchr	Do you think that all the bottle is poison or that all the bottles are the same and somebody's put a drop of poison in one of them?
J	/I think that someone has put¹¹ a drop of poison in that one/
Tchr	Well how could you tell if the bottle had been touched?
J	/It would have fingerprints⁷ on it/ ... they'd wipe³ them off though/
	Pause ....
Tchr	Any other way?
Several Voices	That looks like it – the lid, lid's loose
Tchr	Well have a look at the lids. Pause ....
Tchr	Can you tell which lid is loose?

125

Children's Words

Chorus	That one
A	/That² one/
J	/You can see a finger⁹ mark on/
Tchr	But what about all the other lids?
	Pause ....
Tchr	Have they not been touched?
J	/Them two² haven't/ – they don't look⁹ like it anyway.
Tchr	Stephen?
S	/I think that one 'cos you¹¹ can see there finger marks./
Tchr	We were talking about the lids at the top.
S	er er
Tchr	Jacqueline said you'd be able to see that the lid was loose. Now look at all the lids.
S	/That looks like it's just been er ... screwed² off/
A	/that lid's nearly hanging² off/
	Pause ....
Tchr	Is that likely to be the one with poison in?
A	/Yeh/
	Pause ....
J	/That one's got white² and black things there/
A	/That's got white² things in/you can see white⁹ things in/
Tchr	We've thought about the colour and about the lids. You've still not told me about the lids properly.

Diagnostic teaching

S	/'Cos that's been open³ed by a bottle opener/
Tchr	Have the others been touched?
S & A	/Yeh/
A	/You have to touch th³em to take the lids off/
Tchr	So can we tell with the lid?
A	/They've all³ had them off/
	Pause ....
Tchr	So we can't tell with the colour and we can't tell with the lid. Is there any other way? ... Think of all you've heard about poison or seen on the television?
J	/Drink it ¹⁰.../
Tchr	If you drink it what will happen?
M	/You'll get ⁷poisoned/
A	/(Like)¹ they have (little¹ thingy) magnicope¹⁰/ and the put (li¹ke) it in a thingy⁷/ and they have to look throug⁷h it and they can see all't thingies in it./
Tchr	That's an idea isn't it?
S	/Smell ¹⁰at um/
Tchr	We've thought of a lot of things now
M	/You could tell by¹⁰ t'label if it had any on/
Tchr	Good Marg. Tell me yours again Stephen.
S	/You can sme²ll at um (like ... ¹you can smell)/
Tchr	Go on then.
S	/this o¹¹ne .../
Tchr	Why?

Children's Words

S	/Smells like oránge/²
	Laughter. Others try
Tchr	What does it smell like to you?
M	/Oránge/²
J	(Laughing) /Oránge/²
A	/Oránge/²

....

Tchr	Does that make it poison?
M	/Nó/²
A	/There might have been óran ge in the bottle/³ (Stephen speaks simultaneously)
Tchr	What did you say Stephen?
S	/They all smell like orange/³
Tchr	There's no difference – we can't tell with the smell.
	Pause ....
Tchr	So we've thought about colour, lids and the smell. Any other way you might tell?
A	/Like if there's things in it/¹⁰ (little things in it)¹ ...
Tchr	Any other way?
M	/There's little things in it anyway/⁵
J	/That looks deeper .../²
Tchr	What do you mean deeper?
J	/You can see finger marks there/²
Tchr	You think they are a clue?
S	/I can see finger marks on all of them/³

....

Diagnostic teaching

Tchr   So we can't tell from that

Very long pause ...

Tchr   Sometimes you can smell it, see it, you said you might be able to drink it. I don't think you could drink it ...
Why?

J   /You'd die/

Long pause ...

Tchr   What could you do instead of DRINKING it?
Long pause

A   /Put it on a magniscope and if you see (like) thingies inside of it/

S   /You'll know its poison/

Tchr   Yes but if we haven't got one of those what could we do?

....

Something like DRINK but not take a lot

S   /Just sip it/

....

Tchr   I don't think I'd even sip it.

S   Do something else

J   /I'd just lick it/

A   /I'd put my finger in it/ just get a little bit on my finger and taste it/

Tchr   What might it taste like if it was poison

A   Raw onions

J   /I think it would taste like an orange/because on television it showed (on that that and) them oranges/

Pause ....

Tchr	Showed what?
J	/Poisoned, them² oranges,/ so it might be³ that poison/
Tchr	Mn. We haven't tried tasting it yet. Show me how you would taste it Margaret.
M	/I'd just dip my finger² in like that/
Tchr	Go on. ....
Tchr	Would you taste just one?
M	/Try em³ all/ (trying all bottles)
M	/That one¹¹ . . ./
Tchr	Why?
M	/'Cos that tastes different and⁸ all others taste same/
Tchr	How does that taste?
M	/Horrible²/
Tchr	So do you think that's it?
M	/Might³ be . . ./
Tchr	Well I'll tell you. This poison is so deadly that if you had even tasted it you would have died. So we can't tell by tasting.
J	/No³/
	Very long pause ....
Tchr	Well think of TV films where people are mixing poison – Sometimes something gets knocked over.
A	Like

Diagnostic teaching

M	Wipe it up[2]
J	/Just get a clean[2] cloth/ (If you just put a[1] towel under) /and/ (put some on)/wipe all round[2]/ and put it into[2] a big bucket/
Tchr	And what would that do?

....

Tchr	Suppose I knocked the bottles over ... The liquid in them came on the table. Can you think of what the poison might do that the other won't do?
A	/Just spread[10] it .../
S	/I think it would start[11] burning the table/
J	/It would go[6] all brown/
A	/(like stuff[8] what) if it was on't table[10] you would burn all your finger/
Tchr	Yes poison might burn your finger – might burn your tongue if you taste then.
A	/(Like)[8], like pepper (that's) burns[7] your tongue/
M	/Makes you[7] sneeze/
Tchr	Well let's have just another minute. Now do you really think Margaret that there is poison in one of these bottles?
	Long pause ....
J	/I don't[3]/
S	/I don't[3]/
M	/Yeh/
Tchr	What do you think Antony?
A	/Yeh/

131

Children's Words

S /I think there's[11] none in/

J I think there isn't[11] any cos they all look the same

Tchr All right: Something I said to Margaret should give you the clue.
....
Something I said shows you.
Something Margaret did.

J /Tasting[2] it/

A /Tasting[2] it/
....

Tchr What did I say when she had tasted them all?

M /They're[2] all the same/
....

Tchr What would she be now that she's tasted them all?
Deadly poison

S /She'd be[7] dead/

Table 5 Frequency comparison of speech types used Non-fluent (Poison bottles)

	Maze	Reporting	Reasoning	Personal	Arguing	Collaborating	Recognising principles	Comparing	Justifying	Tentative	Hypothesising	Questioning
Steven	4	8	5	0	0	1	1	0	2	5	4	1
Antony	9	11	3	0	0	0	3	0	1	2	1	0
Margaret	0	6	6	0	0	0	2	1	0	0	1	0
Jacqueline	4	12	3	0	1	1	2	0	2	3	4	0
Total	17	37	17	0	1	2	8	1	5	10	10	1
%	15.7	34.2	15.7	0	0.9	1.3	7.4	0.9	4.6	9.2	9.2	0.9

Diagnostic teaching

| Tchr | Because I said if you even TASTE a little drop. That was the clue. |

....

Transcript Two: Poison bottles

(Discussion among a group of fluent readers)

Lisa	/Smell them/[10]
L	Laughter
Tchr	Go on Lisa explain.
Lisa	/If you take tops off and[10] have a smell the poison might smell/ and you'd be able't tell[3] which it is then/
Tchr	O.K. Go on have a try (Linda smells at all the liquid)

....

Tchr	What do you think poison might smell like?
Lisa	/I don't know/[4]
A	/Horrible/[11]
S	/If . . . (indistinct) – they won't smell/
L	/I think it's that/[11]
Tchr	Why?
Lisa	/Well it smells different[8] to them two/
Tchr	What about the other one?
Lisa	/That smells same[8] as them/That smells[8] different/

....

| Tchr | How does it smell different? |
| Lisa | /Well I don't[3] know . . . (it's got like) . . . /well |

	you can smell something in them but in that it's got a different kind of smell[8]
Tchr	Would that PROVE it was poison?
Lisa	/I think so/[3] mm

Tchr	What do you think about that Simon?
S	/What way do you mean like?/[12]
L	/With your nose/[6] Laughter
Tchr	Well Lisa says that one smells different.

Tchr	Well do any of you think that because it smells different it proves it is poison?
Chorus	No
Tchr	Why not?
S	/Someone could have put something into it that makes it smell differently, but that is not poisonous/[10]

Tchr	So. We can't tell just by smelling. Any other possible way?
S	/Taste it/[10]
A	/That's a bit daft/[3]
Lisa	/kill yourself/[7]
A	/Kill yourself/
Tchr	No. O.K. It's a good idea, a possible way. How would you taste it?

L	/Drink it/[10]
Tchr	But it's poison.
S	/Pu a bit on your finger and lick it/[10]
Tchr	Try that. Go on.
	Giggling
A	/You can't reach it/[6]
L	/You'll be dead/[6]
S	(I hope not)[4]

....

A	/Not clear – like that[2] you said was poison
S	/It tastes like water/[2]
	Tasting
	Pause
Tchr	Have you decided?
S	/I think that one tastes different/[11] because it's more like a sort of stronger[3] taste (like) and water as well/
Tchr	Do any of them taste like poison?
S	/I don't know what poison[3] tastes like so I couldn't say that/
Tchr	Well what would you imagine it tastes like?
S	/Might taste nice/[11]
Tchr	It might, yes . . .
S	/I could imagine it tastes like[3] eggs 'cos I like eggs/
L	/Alcohol/[10]

Children's Words

S	/What kind of alcohol?/[12]

....

Tchr	In fact it could taste like anything.

....

A /Different things taste all right/[3]

Tchr Think of things in the house you've been told not to drink – besides alcohol.

Smiles and giggles

S /T.C.P./[2]

Lisa /Bleach/[11]

Tchr What sort of taste?

A /Horrid/[11]

L /Tangy/[11]

....

A /Acid/[11]

S & A /Burns you/[11]

Tchr So what about those Simon?

S /They don't burn I don't think.[2] /None of them do ... just a funny taste in[2] my mouth now/

Tchr Well does the fact that one tastes different prove its poison?

S & A /No/[3]

Tchr We've not solved the problem.

A /Could be just the flavour/[11]

Tchr Come on be detectives.

S /You could tell like different colours/[10]

A /I'll go for that one 'cos (it) it's not as clear as the others/[8]

136

Diagnostic teaching

S	/That looks a bit more cloudy/
L	/These two tops are more flat than that one/it's cocking up/
Tchr	So what does that prove?
L	/Probably been opened/Might have been opened/
Tchr	But does it prove?
L	/No/
S	/Lift the bottle up and have a look underneath/ cos you'd only have them like that so you'd know which one was poison.
Tchr	The tops: what about the other three tops if you thought that was poison?
A	/Flat on/
L	/They've all been opened/

....

Tchr   Think then – if they've all been opened.

....

S	/They could have put a small bit in/
A	/'Cos if it was all poison it wouldn't look the same/ if it was all poison. It could be a different colour.

....

Tchr	Come on detectives what would they look for?
A	/Fingerprints/
S	/Yeh, I was just going to say/
L	/Well everybody's touched them/
S	/Yeh I (was just er) just remarked/

....

Children's Words

Tchr	Go back and think. We've tried smelling, tasting, fingerprints, lids, any other possible way?
S	/Shaking the bottle up in case[10] anything liked settled/
A	/It would all come[3] out like/
	(Laughter)
Tchr	I don't think that's likely, why not looking at these bottles
A	/They're not[3] fizzy/
S	/You can't see anything[3] on the bottom/
A	/Could be a thicker kind[10] of liquid than the others/
Tchr	By looking can you tell?
A	/No not[3] really/

....

Tchr	Think – monster films – if they spill over, is that a clue for you for something else?
L	/Like spray[7]/no em[7] steam/no smoke[7]/
Lisa	/It would like burn the[11] table and leave a mark/
A	/Sets it on[7] fire/

....

Tchr	Well, have you decided?
L	/I think it's that[11]/
Tchr	Have you got proof?
L	/No[3]/
S	/The only proof is that[3] it smells different and tastes different/

....

Diagnostic teaching

Tchr   You've found that out but does it prove that it's poison?

Chorus   No

Long pause

Tchr   I'll give a final clue, who said that you could taste it?

S   /Mé/

Tchr   Well this poison's so deadly that one drop ...

Chorus   Oh (laughter)

Tchr   ... Would kill you
So which has the poison in?

S   /Nóne of 'em/

....

Tchr   Why?

A   /'Cos it didn't kíll him/

Table 6   Frequency comparison of speech types used

Fluent (poison bottle)

	Maze	Reporting	Reasoning	Personal	Arguing	Collaborating	Recognising principles	Comparing	Justifying	Tentative	Hypothesising	Questioning
Simon	2	3	11	4	0	0	2	1	0	8	1	2
Andrew	1	0	8	0	0	1	7	1	0	2	1	0
Linda	0	0	7	0	0	2	1	1	1	3	2	0
Lisa	1	0	3	1	0	0	3	4	1	2	0	0
Total	4	3	29	5	0	3	13	7	2	15	4	2
%	4.8	3.6	35	6.0	0	3.6	15.7	9.4	2.4	18.1	4.8	2.4

Children's Words

Commentary

It is interesting to note that the non-fluent reading group actually produced a much larger number of utterances than the fluent group though this certainly does not mean that their efforts were superior. For example, the fluent group produced only 4.8% of mazes whereas the figure for the non-fluent group was 15.7% and some of these show just how confused the group became at times despite the efforts of the teacher to lead them to more profitable considerations, e.g. 'because on television it showed on that that and them oranges'.

Since the task is a problem solving one, one would expect a high incidence of utterances of the reasoning, arguing, justifying and hypothesizing type. The non-fluent group in fact had somewhat higher scores on all these classifications with the exception of reasoning. To a degree this could be a fault of the classification system for reasoning could well include the other three types and the reader may well disagree with the way in which the assignment to classes has been made. However, even if one puts all four classes together, the fluent group scored so highly under the reasoning heading that their total for the four classes is almost twice that of the non-fluent group. Possibly it is two uncontrolled variables that have led to this situation: the fluent group could well have a higher level of general ability and by virtue of this and their reading fluency have a better background of relevant knowledge and of this type of task. The non-fluent group certainly appeared happy to report heavily and many of their utterances were repetitions which was not the case in the fluent group.

But it should be borne in mind that most studies of language behaviour have suggested that the reasoning, tentativeness and recognition of principle categories distinguish a rather more advanced stage of language development and thinking than do the other categories.

The non-fluent group discussion was characterized by

other illustrations of their poor language level. The children were very repetitious not merely of ideas but also of vocabulary – for example, the constant recurrence of 'white', 'black' and 'brown' whereas the fluent group use 'clear' and 'cloudy' (the bottles were in fact all filled with clear water). The fluent group also considered smell and taste neither of which were really explored by the non-fluent group.

It is interesting to note the greater effect of both the teacher's promptings and the comments of other children upon the discussions of the fluent group. The non-fluent group seemed largely to ignore what their colleagues had said and simply carry on with their individual comments in an egocentric manner. Equally, the grammar and vocabulary show a much lower level of development. Whether it was lack of attention or simply lack of knowledge, the use of 'magnicope' by one child for 'microscope' remained unchallenged.

It must be remembered that this was an abstract problem and one clear message arises, namely that the non-fluent group need to undertake far more discussions demanding problem solving which have a concrete basis and lie within a background of experience.

The within group differences are small for in each group the performance of the children in terms of type of utterance were remarkably similar. The weaknesses of individuals in both groups in terms of vocabulary and grammar can be seen from the transcripts themselves without the necessity for further comment.

Children's Words

Telling and retelling

These devices present the opportunity to relate the spoken word to real experience, pictures or written language. The range of situations on which the activities can be based is very wide but the following major areas will indicate the possibilities.

Telling

- the recounting of experiences the child has had
- the presentation of information to others
- the oral production of an imaginative situation or
- story of the child's own making.

Retelling

- the composition of a story line based upon a series of pictures (see the example in Chapter 2 based upon the picture story *Fluffy's Aeroplane*)
- the re-expression of a story previously read or heard
- the presentation of information gleaned from one or more written language sources.

The activities help the teacher to observe needs and encourage development in the following areas. Observation is aided if occasionally the activities are recorded on tape and listened to carefully away from the demands of the classroom.

- in picture based activities the child's command of visual perception and orientation can be observed together with the ability to comprehend illustrative material – similar observations can be made among older children based on diagramatic devices and maps.

- the range of the child's vocabulary, i.e. the number of different words used can be observed but it must be remembered that the possible range is proscribed by the nature of the task and any material on which it may be based.

- inadequacies in the range of words employed in certain parts of speech. For example, children in the early stages of language development or those who have a restricted language environment tend to employ only a small number of different adjectives and adverbs.

- the range of types of sentence constructions used, grammatical errors and inability to use appropriately certain tenses or modes of verbs, e.g. a child may be limited to simple subject/verb/object type sentences and only produce longer utterances by connecting a series of such by the word 'and'. It is common also for many children to superimpose the regular verb forms upon irregular verbs, e.g. 'ranned', or 'runned' for 'ran'. And many children at the ten and eleven year old stage find the conditional tense and passive mood difficult to use.

- the ability to present or memorize a sequence of events – for example in a re-telling of the "Gingerbread Man" it is quite common for young children to introduce the various characters in an incorrect order, omit a character or have a character speak the lines associated with another character. Similarly an older child reporting for example an experiment in chemistry may describe the reactions of the elements in an incorrect order.

- the extent to which any retelling is a parroting rather than a re-expression in the child's own words of the author's work. This usually denotes weaknesses in comprehension, in the experiential background of the child or restricted or inhibited use of language.

- the balance given by the child to the main events or ideas of the author in comparison to the subordinate ones. Although this may reveal some lack in comprehension of the author's work or weakness in memorization it may equally point to the child's own purpose in his listening or

Children's Words

reading or betray his preferences and interests, thus providing guidance concerning purpose and content emphases for future work.

- conceptual difficulties may be checked; for example a child may be misled in the meaning of a story by the lack of generalization of his concept of word meaning, e.g. associating the use of 'coat' with human beings rather than animals. Equally a child at the secondary level may reveal that he attaches the same meaning to the terms 'mass' and 'weight'.

The following examples show rather different behaviour observed in three five-year-old children who were asked to retell the illustrated story *Pat's Hat*. The original text is set out below.

Pat's Hat
Pat rat puts on her best hat.
She is going to the shops.

Oh dear! The wind is very strong.
It blows Pat's hat away.

Pat runs after her hat
but the wind is too strong.
She cannot catch it.

Pat's hat blows into a tree
and Pat begins to cry.
'Oh dear, I have lost my best hat.'

Pat rat cannot reach her hat.
She cannot get up the tree.
What can she do?

Pat sat down by the tree
and began to cry again.

Diagnostic teaching

A man came along and said,
'Why are you crying, little rat?'
'Oh please, help me get my best hat
out of the tree,' said Pat.

The man looked up and saw the hat.
He tried to get it down with a stick
but he could not reach it.

Pat rat sat down and began to cry again.
'I will never get my hat back again,'
she cried.
Just then, Sam the dog came along.
'I will help you,' he said.

Sam jumped up.
He jumped again and again
but he could not get Pat's hat.

'Oh dear, I will never get my hat back,'
said Pat.
'The cat will help you,' said Sam.
'The cat can climb into the tree.'

Pat rat did not like the cat.
But the cat helped Pat.
She climbed into the tree
and sent down Pat's hat.

'Thank you,' said Pat.
'I think I like cats now
but I do not like the wind.'
Pat put her best hat back on
and off she went to the shops.

Example Four *Pat's Hat*
The first retelling of the story took place after the boy

concerned had been involved in a small group prediction exercise based upon only the illustrations and followed by his own oral reading of the text. The oral reading had only five incorrect words and two of these were self-corrected which suggested that the oral reading was being undertaken with a reasonable level of comprehension.

Transcript One

C	First she puts the hat on and the . . . the rat puts the hat on
T	And what happens to the hat?
C	It blows away
T	That's right, where does it blow to?
C	A tree
T	Go on, tell me about it
C	A man comes along and he says stop crying, I can get it, but it was too high.
T	That's right, go on . . . Carry on and who comes next?
C	The dog and he says, I can get it and he can't and he says I can't get it so he tries and can't get it so what happens, the cat comes along and tries and she gets it.

Commentary

As far as can be ascertained this was the first occasion on which this boy had been asked to retell a story which he had previously read. Accordingly he was allowed to turn the pages of the book during the retelling and glance at the illustrations. Memory was not therefore a major part of the task and as the illustrations had previously been discussed at length no difficulties arose here in the perception or comprehension of the picture.

The child started haltingly and needed a good deal of prompting by the teacher to get the idea. When he begins to see what is expected the remainder of the story is given in a rush and sentence construction tends to be forgotten.

The retelling is a minimal summary of the main events. Not only are all the supporting details omitted, but he misses out most of the conversation, the nature of the efforts made by the various characters to reach the hat and the cause and effect relationships within the story. The child is obviously capable of using quite complicated sentence constructions but probably owing to the unfamiliarity of the exercise does not express the story line in a way that would make it enjoyable for any other child to listen to. There is certainly no elaboration despite the extensive discussion of the story in which the child had originally been involved.

Clearly the boy needs much more practice in this type of activity and in the first instance far more questions from the teacher to lead him to a fuller account of the original. One useful way of introducing somewhat inhibited children to this type of activity is to allow them to retell a well-loved and often-read story to a younger child.

The second retelling by a girl took place after the book had been read silently followed by the oral reading of it to the teacher. On this occasion the child did not have the book to refer to during the retelling. The retelling was undertaken into a tape recorder with no one else present. The oral reading of the story had contained seven incorrect words and was read with very little expression – which seemed a little surprising as it was a prepared reading.

Transcript Two

One day Pat wants to go to the shops so she puts her hat on and gets her bag. Pat's hat goes into a tree. Pat runs after her but cannot catch it. Pat begins to cry. Pat jumps but cannot get her hat. Pat sits down to cry again. Pat cries and cries. Then Sam the dog comes. 'Oh I will never get my hat' says Pat. 'Sam can help you' says Sam. Sam jumps and jumps. She cannot get the hat. Pat cries and cries. Pat asks a man to help. The man tries with a stick. He cannot get the hat. Pat cries and cries. Then a cat climbs the tree and gets Pat's hat. Pat likes Cat.

Commentary

This is obviously a much fuller retelling than the previous example. The girl here certainly has the basic idea of the nature of the task and includes the major events. In fact had the task been to present a summary of the story it could be said that she had given the main ideas though there are weaknesses in terms of the memorization of the sequence of the events.

More interesting, however, is the resistance to the use of pronouns which makes the retelling rather choppy and may have added to the problems of memorizing the sequence of the story. The few pronouns included do suggest that there is a small difficulty not uncommon at this age in relating a pronoun to its noun referent when the two are in separate sentences.

This retelling misses many of the cause and effect elements of the story thus suggesting rather a shallow reading. Also the vocabulary of the original is so much more extensive and varied than the girl's effort. This is seen most strongly in the complete absence of any attempt at description. It could be that she prefers the action to the description but equally it could suggest a limited vocabulary, which further observation in fact confirmed. A further sign of this child's linguistic immaturity is her presentation of the story in entirely present tense form.

The third child who undertook this task was of Asian parents but was herself born in Britain. The presentation procedure was the same as in the previous example. In her oral reading she made only three errors and read with reasonable expression.

Transcript

Pat Rat is going to the shops. She is putting on her best hat and is getting her shopping bag. She is going out but the wind is blowing her very strongly. It blows her hat off. Pat chases after her hat but the wind is very strong and she cannot catch it. Her hat is being caught in a tree. Pat jumped up but she could not get her hat and she bagan to cry. A man is coming along and he says 'Why do you be crying?' Pat is saying 'Please do help me, my lovely hat is for being caughted in the tree.' The man tried to get the hat with his stick but he couldn't reach it. Pat was beginning for to think that there was no way she would get back her hat. Sam the dog is to be trying to help her. He jumped and jumpted but he is not for going to get it either. 'We must be after fetching the cat' said Sam. 'Cats are very good at climbing trees.' But Pat was worried for rats are not for being friendly with cats. The cat came along and she did climb the tree and is knocking down Pat's pretty hat. Pat says 'Thank you very much rat. I am for liking of cats now but I am hating nasty winds.'

Commentary

In terms of comprehension, vocabulary, memorization of the sequence and portrayal of the mood of the original story this is an excellent retelling. Most of the cause and effect relationships are established and extra vocabulary introduced which demonstrates the extent to which the story was comprehended and internalized. There is, however, a peculiar mixture of grammatical usage centralized around the verb forms. This appears to be the result of the language influences of her Asian parentage and local dialect with some evidence also of a tendency to persist in forcing verbs to conform to one particular model in the way they are conjugated. Such difficulties could inhibit future comprehension growth and the teacher must endeavour to present a consistent model for the child to copy.

Informal reading inventories

The use of informal reading inventories expanded during the late 1950s but in those early years were very narrow in concept. They gained popularity because they tested children on the material they were using rather than making decisions concerning the material to be used on the basis of a score within a standardized test. In origin they simply aimed to match child and text appropriately. For this purpose it seemed important only to establish recognition of the vocabulary and ability to comprehend the content of the early pages of a book in order to feel that the child could use a particular book to advantage. This procedure has been criticized for often a single passage lifted from the book is a poor reflection of the book as a whole in terms of the variability of the level of difficulty within the book.

One positive service established by the early work in this field was the suggestion that reading attainment was not a one level matter. Rather, in relation to any given reading material a reader might perform within a range of levels described as *independent*, *instructional* and *frustration* levels.

Independent level – ability to read a passage with 95% accuracy in reading the words and 100% ability to comprehend the material.

Instructional level – 90 to 95% word accuracy and more than 75% comprehension.

Frustration level – less than 90% word accuracy and not more than 50% comprehension.

The percentages are only to be considered as rough averages. As a general rule the child who is making good progress will have a much greater range between the level of material which he can read at the independent level and that which he finds frustrating than will the child who is making little progress.

In the original form the informal reading inventory consisted of a measure of words read correctly in a passage and the number of questions on its content answered correctly. It would seem obvious that such a narrow appraisal could supply very little information to the teacher as regards the nature of the abilities and needs of the child and must largely ignore the attitudes and purposes which can influence both motivation and performance.

The remainder of the devices described in this book are based upon the idea of the informal reading inventory but it will be seen that they are more easily related to the wider view of reading outlined in chapter 1. Equally, the range suggested makes it possible to observe all the language arts, and not merely reading, in the context of the total curriculum.

Oral reading miscue analysis

Oral reading by the child to the teacher frequently takes place in the early years of schooling but tends to be little used later except in the case of children with considerable reading difficulty. Possibly oral reading is overused in the early stages with the consequence that the child may come to view reading as being concerned with the accurate reproduction of sounds rather than the appreciation of meaning and so be unable to read at a pace other than that at which she speaks. Even so it would be helpful to have occasional oral reading sessions for older children to check upon any difficulties in vocabulary or the ability to interpret meaning through the appropriate use of pause, emphasis and intonation.

The differences between oral and silent reading behaviour need to be clearly appreciated for otherwise too much may be inferred concerning the child's reading when undertaking oral reading miscue analysis. In oral reading the demand is for a fluent presentation to an audience and accuracy in the presentation and sequencing of the author's words. In silent reading, on the other hand, the way in which the material is read is controlled by the reader's purposes concerning the outcomes he wishes to gain. The reader may return to check whether he had appreciated the meaning of a word or phrase whereas in oral reading this breaks the sequence. The pace of oral reading permits of very little variation whereas in silent reading the pace can be varied according to the level of difficulty, type of material and the purposes of the reader. In silent reading there can be greater attention to meaning and this can have an effect upon the level of word identification. In oral reading there is a tendency to depend rather more heavily upon the memorization of the spelling patterns of words and the use of sound/symbol association whereas in silent reading the concentration is perhaps more upon the use of context as an aid to word identification.

To some extent this imbalance can be overcome by having some oral reading sessions where the passage to be read has previously been prepared by the child. This can be done by simply looking at any illustrations, discussing them or the topic covered by the passage, by prior silent reading or the provision of questions for which answers are to be sought in the passage.

Oral reading miscue analysis may on first sight seem to be time consuming. In fact the miscues take no longer to collect than it does for the child to read, and with practice the classification and interpretation takes only a few minutes. Prior to becoming proficient in using the technique, it is helpful to tape record examples and carry out the annotation without the child being present. The following symbols are suggested for ease of recording upon the actual text.

Omissions: There was once (a) dragon

Insertions: a dragon ∧ who lived

Children's Words

Pauses:	When the children // from
Words sounded out:	w e n t
	ran ---
Substitutions:	went up the hill
Repetitions:	dr drag ⌒dragon
Corrections:	c up up and ⌒down went the -----

In summary the following points will be helpful in making full use of oral reading miscue analysis.

1. The work of any child should be examined together with his performance in other types of situation, e.g. cloze procedure.

2. Best results (from the point of view of valid information for teaching) are gained if the reading is undertaken at roughly the instructional level. In the case of young children and children experiencing reading problems the tendency is to resort to rather different reading strategies if the difficulty level of the passage moves towards the child's frustration level. Even fluent reading adults tend to use phonics far more heavily on a passage which is outside their normal experience.

3. Observations should take place periodically – any one occasion may not produce the normal behaviour of the child or give opportunity to observe certain needs. A dossier needs to be built up over a period if the effort made is to produce accurate helpful results and so benefit the child and teacher in saving time through the precise selection of teaching strategies and learning activities.

4. Some thirty miscues on any one occasion should be collected if an analysis is to be worthwhile.

Diagnostic teaching

5 Observations should take place on a variety of materials. For example, some children produce markedly different behaviour on story and informational materials.

6 Undue importance should not be placed upon any one miscue for it may not be typical behaviour. Action should only be undertaken when several similar examples are found which suggest a pattern of need. This problem will rarely occur in a prepared passage.

7 Miscues must be looked at closely and all possible reasons for them considered before a judgement is made. They need to be looked at in terms of the error, the context, the expression being given to the passage, relationships with other errors and the possibility that they may arise from a lack of understanding of the meaning of other words which may have been read correctly. Many solutions can be gained by asking a child to listen to a tape of his own reading and being allowed to correct his miscues or to explain his difficulties.

Example Five *There was once a dragon*

Transcript

```
                one           a                    the
There was once  (a)  dragon ∧ who lived // in a cave //
  one one       said  the morning    went        lone
On the // side of a mountain. He was very lonely. He

wanted someone // to // talk to. When the children //
             vllg   comed    a big monster
from // the // village came up the/ mountain to play, the
                  over     on              ∧        just
dragon // rushed out // of // his // cave to // join them.
```

Commentary

John reads in a slow deliberate cumbersome style. He is making an effort but needs much more specific help and

Table 7 Linear analysis ('There was once a dragon')

Text word	Miscue	Grapho-phonic similarity	Meaning	Function
once	one	√	X	X
a	the	X	√	√
on	one	√	X	X
side	said	√	X	X
mountain	morning	√	X	√
was	went	√	X	√
lonely	lone	√	√	X
village	villg	√	X	X
came	comed	√	√	√
the	a	X	√	√
mountain	monster	√	X	√
out	over	√	X	√
of	on	√	X	X
join	just	√	X	X

general experience to extend his skills and to generate confidence.

He is not seeing the text as a series of word sequences and sentences from which he has to get meaning, to enjoy the unfolding story, e.g. the misplacement of 'a' in the first line, and he has no strategy to deal with a text that is obviously not making sense to him.

Indeed, his substitution of 'comed' for 'came' confirms his general immaturity not only in decoding the written word but in oral language too. It would seem that he is being overchallenged at the moment and would benefit from general support to his word attack skills at a lower level of reading difficulty.

Example Six *Kes*
In the example from a reading of *Kes* which follows, comprehension questions were also set to see if these would provide further insights into the reader's behaviour.

Transcript

    The wind had dropped. It was starting to rain. Big
spots dotted the asphalt like pennies from heaven. On
top of the cycle shed a black cat froze in mid-stride and
stared down at him. When he shut the door the noise
and movement sent it silently down the grain of the tin
and out of / sight down the back of the shed.

    It was quiet without the wind. No birds sang, and the
singing had stopped in school. There was no sound from/
/ the school. Billy stood back in the doorway listening,
and watching the /back corner of the shed. Nothing
happened. So he ran across and/had/a look. The cat had
gone. On the roof of the shed the rain drops were /
quickening like a heartbeat. The sound / developed / into
a solo, and water began to trickle down the tin, bringing
up the rust, copper and orange. Billy turned round and
/sprinted. Round the corner of the building, straight in
through the toilets and into the / corridor. Empty. The
first classroom he looked into was empty. The second was
/ occupied. He stared in until he attracted everyone's
attention, and the teacher came / rushing to the door.

    'What's / the / matter, / Casper? What are you / looking
at?'

'What time / is it, Sir?'

'Time! Never / mind / the / time / lad! What do you want?'

He stepped down / the corridor. Billy stepped back.

'Is / this/ 3B, Sir?'

'No, it isn't 3B, why?'

'I thought it wa'. I've got a message for / 'em.'

'Well get to the office then.'

'Why, are they in there, / Sir?'

'No, to find out where they are, you fool! Ask the secretary to look at the timetable.'

'Yes, Sir. I forgot.'

'You will forget, / lad, if you come / disturbing me again like that.'

He/banged the door and frowned/his way/across to his desk. He was still / frowning when he / resumed the lesson, two / vertical //frowns between his eyes. Billy walked slowly by and looked into the next room. A class was working. He / dodged back/out of sight and stood between the two rooms with his back to the radiator, glancing / continually right and left, up and down the corridor.

Diagnostic teaching

Questions

Q.1 Can you just tell me what that bit's about? [inferring main ideas]

A. It's about Billy . . . he's skiving from his lessons . . . and he's looking in all't classrooms for his own lesson. It's raining outside and . . . on't bicycle shed roof, there's all water, trickling off.

Q.2 Why does he say he's got a message for 3B? [motivation of characters]

A. I don't know

Q.3 Do you think he had a message for 3B? [motivation of character]

A. No

Q.4 Then why would he say that? [predicting outcomes]

A. So's he can . . . so's he doesn't get done off teachers

Q.5 Why would he get done [inferring cause and effect relationships]

A. For skiving out of the lessons

Q.6 How does the teacher in the classroom treat Billy? [inferring character traits]

A. He's mad with him . . . for coming in his lesson

Commentary

This boy's overall level of performance indicated that he was reading a text at his instructional level, i.e. with an error rate of approximately 10 per cent of the total number of words.

His replies to the comprehension questions showed that although his grouping and phrasing in reading the passage were on the whole good and he attempted to correct some of his errors on the basis of the meaning of the surrounding text, his overall appraisal and memorization of the passage were somewhat weak. From the word difficulty experienced, the phrasing and answers to the questions, there is some evidence that when something doesn't make sense to him he forgets it and reads on. This may well arise from a rather poor linguistic background, lower than average

Table 8 Linear analysis (*Kes*)

Text word	Miscue	Grapho-phonic similarity	Meaning	Function
dotted	dropped	√	√	√
asphalt	aspart	√	X	X
pennies	pencils	√	X	√
mid-stride	mid-strade	√	X	√
stared	started	√	X	√
silently	silent	√	X	X
back	black	√	X	
shed	sheet	√	X	√
quiet	quite	√	X	X
from	of	√	X	√
solo	sole	√	x	√
straight	started star..ing	√	X	X
through	thought	√	X	X
stared	started	√	X	√
wa'	was	√	√	√
You	Look	X	X	X
frowning	forwon	√	X	X
frowns	frons	√	X	X
was	of	X	X	X
radiator	radiate	√	X	X
continually	continuously	√	√	√

development of concepts and attitudes or a narrow view of reading as being a word identification exercise. His ability to appraise sound/symbol relationships, however, and memorize the spelling of words is reasonable. The majority of his miscues were close in spelling and sound to the author's words but often he failed to pick up the crucial one, e.g. 'through' for 'though'. This is no doubt due to his resort to phonics for clues to an unknown word more frequently than endeavouring to appraise syntax and meaning. Again, where a word was eventually given after difficulty, its match was to the preceding context, rarely to the following part of a sentence. It would seem that further investigation in terms of the use of cloze procedure might throw light on his reading and that his use of context cues and comprehension may be aided by discussions based on cloze or prediction exercises.

Cloze procedure

Cloze procedure is a device where words are omitted from a text and the child endeavours to complete the gaps. It is not a truly realistic task as the child can only complete each space by reference to the syntax and meaning of the context. Perhaps this brings out a greater difference in behaviour than that of tackling an unknown word in a complete passage, for in normal reading the task is one of recognition whilst in cloze it is one of production. It does, however, emphasize the usage of context and enables the child to develop his skills in locating cues, in this way balancing to some extent the leaning of miscue analysis towards an observation of the use of grapho/phonic cues. Equally, it provides the teacher with an opportunity to observe and teach to, the child's needs.

Passages for such exercises can be prepared by sticking masking tape over the words to be deleted within a book or by typing the text out again with appropriate spaces. The initial ideas of how to approach such exercises can be developed by the use of pictorial comic strips where the child has to suggest what might happen in the missing pictures.

The following are some forms of cloze procedure which may be found helpful.

- deleting words at random or say every seventh word and representing them by a standard length space

- deleting particular parts of speech, e.g. adjectives

These two procedures have proved to be most helpful for cooperative or postcompletion discussions (see pp. 52–55).

- leaving a letter or letters in each word space to give the child some grapho-phonic information

- inserting dashes to indicate the number of letters in the word.

The latter two procedures constrain the possible responses a child may make and draw attention to word form rather than function and meaning. Also there is an added tendency for a reply to fall into either right or wrong categories whereas in the former two approaches the responses can be thought of in terms of levels of appropriateness. The slow-learning child particularly appreciates this change from most other classroom marking systems and is thrilled when it is suggested that his word may be a better choice than the one the author actually used.

In all the forms of cloze procedure a clear beginning is essential. Passages selected should either be complete in themselves or be the opening part of a story or section of an informational text so that any background information necessary for their completion should be generalized knowledge rather than specific references to an earlier passage. It is also a good idea to provide a few sentences at the beginning of the passage before the deletion of words commences. For any reasonable analysis or discussion to take place there need to be twenty-five or more deletions to which the child must respond. Frequently children respond in very different ways to different types of text and at the secondary level particularly it is important to compare the pattern of responses in the various types of media and subject texts. The frequency of deletions will interact with the type of deletion and the level of development of the children. A rough guide, however, would be not more than one in ten running words for children of seven years or below, seven to ten years a deletion rate of one word in seven and from eleven years onwards, one word in five running words.

All four types of deletion listed above permit of analysis by the following suggested model. The analysis here would be on the basis of classifying the individual's written responses to the deletions within a passage.

Descriptions of analysis categories

1 Author's original word replaced. Experience suggests that if 45 per cent or more of the gaps are completed by the child with the author's original words then the child has achieved a very good level of comprehension of the passage and has used his context cues very well.

2 A synonym of the author's word. If the child reaches over 80 per cent of clozures in these first two categories then his level of comprehension and context cueing within the passage is at a high level and he could be given passages of much greater difficulty in order to discover his needs for further teaching to take place.

3 Not in tune with the author's overall meaning but grammatically correct.

4 Meaningful in relation to the preceding part of the sentence but not to the section which follows.

5 Meaningful to the following part of the sentence but not to the preceding material.

6 Not meaningful but grammatically appropriate to the preceding part of the sentence but not to the later part.

7 Not meaningful but grammatically appropriate to the following part of the sentence though not to the preceding matter.

Example Seven *Wilbur's new home*
(The following passage is one from which verbs or parts of verbs have been deleted and is analysed in terms of the above model. The level would be that of the average eleven-year-old child.)

Wilbur's new home was in the lower part of the barn directly underneath the cows. Mr Wilson knew that a manure pile was a good place to keep a young pig. Pigs need warmth, and it was warm and comfortable down there in the barn cellar on the south side.

Carol came almost every day to visit him. She *saw* (found) an old milking stool that had *seen* (been) discarded and she placed the stool in the sheepfold next to Wilbur's pen. There she *sat* ✓ quietly during the long afternoons, *sitting* (thinking) and listening and watching Wilbur. The sheep soon *got* ✓ to know her and trust her. So *then* (did) did the geese, who lived with the sheep. All the animals *knew* (trusted) her because she was so quiet and friendly. Mr Wilson *had* (did) not allow Carol to take Wilbur out, neither did he *let* (allow) her to get into the pigpen. But he *would* (did) tell Carol that she could sit on the stool and *watch* ✓ Wilbur as long as she wanted to. It *made* ✓ her happy just to be near the pig, and it made Wilbur happy to *think* (know) that she was sitting there, right outside his pen. But Wilbur never *had*✓ any fun. He had no walks, no rides, no swims.

One afternoon in June, when Wilbur *was*✓ almost two months old, he *ran* [wandered] out into his small yard outside the barn. Carol had not *come* [arrived] for her usual visit and Wilbur *sat* [stood] in the sun feeling lonely and bored.

'There's never anything to *do*✓ around here', he thought. He *went* [walked] slowly to his food trough and *looked* [sniffed] to see if anything had been overlooked at lunch. He *ate* [ate] a small strip of potato skin and *liked* [found] it. His back itched, so he *scratched* [leaned] against the fence and rubbed against the boards. When he *finished* [tired] of this, he walked indoors, *rushed* [climbed] to the top of the manure pile, and sat down. He didn't *want* [feel] like going to sleep.

Commentary

Out of 27 spaces the child selects the author's original word on 7 occasions. This is a rate of only 26 per cent which suggests that the passage is a little on the difficult side for him. When acceptable replacements are added, the total is 16 out of 27, i.e. 59 per cent, again on the low side despite very generous marking. However, it should be noted that in gaining the best information from the use of cloze procedure it is best to pitch the passage level slightly harder than the child's instructional level. This is particularly important

Table 9 Analysis categories (Wilbur's new home)

		2	3	4	5	6	7
found	saw	√					
seen	been			√			√
thinking	sitting	√					
did	then			√			
trusted	knew		√				
did	had			√			
allow	let	√					
did	would	√					
know	think	√					
wandered	ran	√					
arrived	come	√					
stood	sat	√					
walked	went	√					
sniffed	looked		√				
found	ate		√				
ate	liked		√				
leaned	scratched				√		
tired	finished				√		
climbed	rushed		√				
feel	want				√		

if a discussion approach is to be used.

In looking at the non-acceptable words a little information may be gained about the child's strategies. In using 'then' for 'did' the response appears to conform to the immediate reaction to normal speech patterns, as a word that often follows 'so' in the child's experience. This sort of patterning which inevitably relates the word replaced more heavily to the preceding matter rather than to the following is a regular feature of the child's approach. He appears therefore to be reading chronologically and though his responses show that he has a reasonable grasp of the overall meaning of the passage, he seems happy to forget his responses immediately each one has been made and does not return to reconsider them. One can only assume that this type of behaviour would be a feature of his normal oral and silent reading and may well have developed through an over-concentration upon oral reading in the past.

The usual reason for presenting a passage with verbs deleted is to examine the use of the forms and tenses of verbs. In this connection the substitution of 'then' for 'did' may suggest a lack of knowledge of sentence construction in relation to verbs but there is no other evidence to confirm this – it is the only occasion that he responded with a word other than a verb.

Such an analysis is obviously strictly limited. Even when interpreted with insight in terms of a detailed knowledge of the child, the result only implies the strategies the child used and cannot describe them with any real certainty. The teacher has to know the actual thinking which the child employed and this is where discussion is so important. Two approaches to discussion of cloze passages have been found helpful both in terms of the observation and the development of the child's use of context cues.

1 Two children work together to complete a passage, agreeing a response and the reasons for its applicability prior to completing each gap in the passage.

2 Individuals complete a cloze passage as a written exercise after which they have two discussion sessions:

   (a) a discussion in which they compare responses and agree upon the best word for each gap. Here they are discussing broad areas of meaning and grammatical acceptability.
   (b) a further discussion where the children's agreed words are compared with the ones the author used originally. Here the discussion considers author intent, shades of meaning and emphasis and qualities of style.

Such discussions lead to a greater opportunity for the teacher to observe the children's thinking, language usage and conceptual development in relation to their ability to use context cues.

Reading-thinking activities

It was noted earlier that this general heading covers a variety of discussion activities which can be employed in relation to pictures and the analysis or creation of written material in a thoughtful and logical manner. Indeed the earlier language discussions and cloze procedure could be classified under this heading also, but it is introduced here in relation to two specific types of discussion, namely prediction and sequencing.

Within a *reading-thinking* activity the teacher may observe many of the items which have already been covered such as extent of vocabulary, grammatical knowledge, word identification and the ability to use context clues. In any activity being used as a basis for informal observation it is useful to focus attention on particular abilities rather than try to observe all factors on one occasion.

Prediction exercises are particularly helpful in the observation of comprehension development. The following areas are those which may not have been analysed by the previous activities discussed.

1. general conceptual development especially as it affects comprehension of ideas and word meanings

2. the ability to deal with idioms and figurative language

3. the ability to recognize the structure of a passage and how all the elements cohere together into a meaningful whole

4. the recognition of main and subordinate ideas

5. the ability to detect bias and prejudice within an author's work

6. the use of reasoning to reach conclusions and make decisions

Example Eight is one type of cooperative discussion. A short story has been split into episodes, three in this case.

Diagnostic teaching

The children read the first episode silently then come together in a small group of four or five to discuss what they have read. The idea is that by an appreciation of the clues within the passage read they should draw conclusions concerning what they feel will happen next. Any suggestion made must be supported by a reasoned argument and the other members of the group normally challenge the suggestion, again bringing any evidence of a different possibility. After each such silently read episode the children meet again for a similar discussion, erecting new hypotheses and giving reasons for any earlier suggestions which new evidence demands they must reject.

Discussions of this type can take place at any stage of school life. It has been found that the inability to logically consider other points of view only disappears when children are regularly challenged by an approach such as this. If practice starts early it is much easier to overcome egocentric behaviour and biassed responses than when children are not asked to join in this type of activity until the secondary school stage.

The material needs to be carefully selected if the discussions are to be revealing. In general it is best to choose material slightly more difficult than the current instructional level of the children. Material which has the characteristics of the detective-type novel brings the best results for it usually provides for a number of possible solutions to the cause and effect relationships.

In the early stages the teacher should be present at all such discussions so that the children master the basic techniques. At a later stage many such discussions can be organized without the teacher as leader. In either case the discussions can be taped for the purposes of diagnosis. In the teacher-led discussions the teacher must endeavour to ensure that any questions he poses are not over directive. They should be as neutral and open as possible and framed to help the children consider all the alternatives, rather than concentrate the children's attention upon those elements known to be most fruitful. If children are to learn the analytic techniques involved it is necessary for them to have the experience of controlling the weighting of the discussion. If the teacher feels this is difficult it is useful to gain practice by asking a colleague to select the material for use so enabling the teacher to read the episodes in the same timing as the children. Thus the teacher is in the same problem solving situation as the children in the group and has only their own background knowledge and reasoning to guide the search for a solution.

In the following example of such a discussion the material had been written by the teacher leading it. The group consisted of five nine to ten-year old children of very slightly above average reading ability. This was only their second attempt at this type of activity. The story as a whole has a readability level of about the average for twelve-year-old children. Only the first episode and the discussion which immediately followed it are quoted here.

Example Eight *The fight for freedom*

The stout rope was still holding. She could feel it gradually softening and stretching. It had been a strong rope once, but now it was frayed in parts and the dew was seeping into the worn strands. She knew that where the rope stretched was its weakest part and strained harder than ever to stretch the rope still further.

Insects buzzed hungrily round her head and particularly where the rope, which passed round her neck, had chafed the skin and drawn blood. She wondered how much longer it would take to free herself from the rope and escape from her enemy, now lying peacefully asleep by the fire.

The pain in her leg, where she had been wounded, was agonizing. Every movement she made to free herself seemed to bring new waves of pain to her tortured body. She felt herself growing weaker and dropped against the rough bank unconscious!

Struggling back from her coma she attacked the rope again. Bending her head round, she felt her sharp teeth close over the rope and bit deeply into it. All through the night she continued to struggle. Soon her mouth, tongue and teeth were torn and sore but the rope seemed weaker after each attack – she was sure of that!

Her breathing sounded heavy, she was panting with the effort she was making and, all the time, the rope was biting deeper into the soft coat of her neck. The pain from her wound and her efforts to free herself seemed to drive her into the black depths of unconsciousness time and time again, but each time she recovered and attacked the rope again.

Transcript of discussion

Tchr	Now then, you have just read the first sheet of the first page of this story. What do you think is going to happen now? Jimmy
'A'	Sir . . . sir, every time sshe recovers from bit biting the r.rope she'll bite bite again and get free.
Tchr	Who's this she?
'A'	Sir, its a w.woman been cap.captured by some enemies and the. they've put this rope round her and she's trying to bi.bite it and m.make it free and try and get away.
Tchr	I see. Right, that's a good idea – what does Marshall think?
'B'	Sir, I think the same but I think it's a dog.
Tchr	You think it's a dog – what makes you think its a dog, Marshall?
'B'	Well sir, I when he said a woman trying to bite

	through the ropes sir, I don't think a woman would try to bite through rope.
'A'	I would
Tchr	Well, you've both got your own ideas. That's from what you've read there. What about you Kath?
'C'	Sir, I think it's a dog as well
Tchr	You think it's a dog as well . . .
?	Sir
Tchr	What, what makes you think its a dog?
'C'	Er . . .
Tchr	Anything in particular?
'C'	Sir, when it said er something about her er neck
Tchr	When he said something about her neck.
'B'	Dogs don't have necks and
'A'	Dogs don't have c.coats
Tchr	Now just a minute, now just a minute. Let's see what my friend Susie has to say.
'D'	Sir, I think it might be erm a woman and she's trying to get free from c, all tied up against a pole and, and she she does get free and falls to the ground unconscious.
Tchr	You think she's tied up against a pole. What makes you think she's tied up against a pole?
Tchr	Whereabouts do you think she is now.
'E'	Sir, sir,
Tchr	Have you any idea? . . .

Diagnostic teaching

Tchr	Yes David.
'E'	On a ship
'A'	Sir
Tchr	What makes you think she's on a ship, David?
'E'	Sir, Sir, cos it says something about water
Tchr	Yes, there is something about water.
'B'	Where?
'A'	I can see it.
Tchr	Well can you just read out where it says that, David, for me?

....

'E'	I think it says water is safe
'A'	Oh aye, yes, the pain in her leg where she had been wounded w.was agonizing every movement she made to free herself seemed to bring new waves of pain to her tortured body.
Tchr	Oh, I see what you're getting at.
Tchr	Marshall, yes.
'B'	Sir, I still think it's a dog because it says h.her breathing sounded heavy she was panting with the effort.
Tchr	So you still . . . this makes you feel that that it's definitely a dog. Well now I did ask another question. Some of you think it's a dog and some of you think it's a woman but whereabouts do you think this dog or this woman is. Is there anything (SIR) is there anything there to tell us that m.might tell us. Yes Jimmy.
'A'	Sir, in a a German camp

173

Tchr	In a German camp.
'A'	Ye a a sort . . . of soleri con.confinement and she ti.tied to a post or something and she she's trying to bite to bite her way out bite bite the rope and then get away
Tchr	This was . . . that page gives you the, the out . . . picture, picture of somebody in a concentration camp.
'A'	The enemy was sssiting by the fire
'B'	Yes sir
Tchr	Yes alright, Kath
'C'	I think it's a dog because it says the soft coat of her neck.
Tchr	Yes . . . You're losing the question now the question I did ask was where do you think they are? Where do you think that she and the enemy are? Could you sort of narrow the area of where they are, somebody said they are on the sea another one, Jimmy here, said that they are in a concentration camp. Where would you think they are?
'C'	Sir, I think they are on the sea as well.
Tchr	You would think they are on the sea too. Marshall?
'B'	Sir I think her enemy was a dog because it says and escaped from her enemy now lying peacefully asleep by the fire.
'A'	Sir Sir
'B'	I think it would be a person lying by the fire
Tchr	You don't think it would be a person lying by the fire?

Diagnostic teaching

'B' I think her enemies are a dog

'E' Sir

Tchr I see. Let Susan have a turn, David, Susan say something.

'D' Sir, I think that ther m . . . enemy that's lying by the fire asleep might be a dog.

Tchr You think the enemy might be a dog?

'A' Sir

Tchr And what about the she . . . you still think that's going to be a woman?

'D' Yes sir, I think that some people made the dog stay there.

Tchr Oh I see, yes . . . well that's fine.

'E' Sir, I think that they're they're on this ship and and this pole and that sir, she's tied up and sir but this woman's tied up and this dog's biting her mouth. This dog's quite a ———— (??)

Tchr If you look at that second paragraph though David, you know it does say somebody lying peacefully asleep by the fire . . . does it . . . you still think that this is on board a ship?

Commentary

The above discussion transcript demonstrates many needs of the children within the group which may not have been discovered through oral reading or the asking of comprehension questions or the use of cloze procedure for all these devices focus attention upon elements preselected by the author or teacher. Here the children reveal their appreciation of and response to the text and thus select those elements which attract them or they feel are most related to their purposes.

For example one child believes the situation of the story is on board a ship despite the author's attempt to create the atmosphere of a jungle. On being asked to provide his evidence he points out the metaphor 'waves of pain'. The problem here is probably two-fold. Young children are confused by metaphors unless they have met them frequently and this child definitely does not understand this particular one. Again the teacher has pushed the children rather hard to put the story into its situational context and instead of looking for a number of clues towards this end the child responds with one element of the text only and ignores all other clues. This is a common tendency and one which is often encouraged rather than discouraged by comprehension questions.

Another child in relation to this same point decides on a concentration camp situation. There are a few clues he combines here, e.g. 'wounded', 'tied up', 'enemy', etc., but he is really responding in terms of his recent background experience and superimposing that upon the story. At the time the discussion took place a number of television series were running on the subject of prisoner of war camps.

The other major area of difficulty shown by the children is the way in which narrowness in their concepts of word meaning limits their comprehension. It must be a dog because it is panting and whoever is lying in front of the fire must be a dog because human beings go to bed to do that sort of thing.

The great value of the particular prediction technique is that the teacher stores up all these misapprehensions and brings them back into the discussion of later episodes when the children have more information to help them unravel their mistaken ideas.

Not until the third and final episode is read do the children learn that the 'she' was in fact a leopard, who had been caught by a hunter more than once. Once again she finally escapes from him. By the end of the second episode, however, the children had reached agreement that the 'he' was a hunter and all but one that the 'she' was an animal who had been captured, possibly for transportation to a zoo.

Whereas oral reading and cloze procedure tend to lead children to a concentration on individual words and small parts of text, the advantage of story prediction activity is that much longer stretches of texts are studied as a cohesive unit. This ability becomes very important in any reading for study purposes but equally has a carry over to the appreciation and understanding of spoken language.

Sequencing activities can be designed around a variety of picture sequences such as comic strip stories, pictures depicting actions or processes and texts of almost any type. They are particularly helpful, however, in helping children establish the knowledge, concepts, the manner of thinking and type of language appropriate to the different subject areas. Whereas on some occasions prediction activities emphasize a general impression of the author's meaning and intention, sequencing activities demand attention to detail, very thorough comprehension and conceptual understanding.

Example Nine *The working of an engine*
A group of thirteen-year-old slow learners undertaking a study of cars were given the following summary list of the sequence of events within a four stroke engine together with four simple illustrations equally presented in random order. The group had to place the sentences and illustrations in the correct order as a cooperative exercise. This type of discussion appears to work best with somewhat smaller groups than prediction activities and either two or three children seems ideal. The number alongside each sentence denotes the correct position of each of the ten sentences.

It explodes and pushes the piston down	7
The first stroke opens the inlet valve	1

It presses the petrol and air into a small space	5
The piston moves up again	8
The cycle starts again	10
When the piston is down the valve shuts	3
It pushes waste gases through the open exhaust valve	9
A spark lights this	6
On the second stroke the piston moves up	4
The piston moves down sucking in petrol and air	2

The children were able finally to complete both exercises correctly but *en route* revealed a number of difficulties some of which they were able to solve within the group. A few, however, needed further questioning from the teacher before understanding was achieved.

Firstly they proved to be rather poor at recognizing and using as preliminary organizers any of the obvious language signals. By ignoring them they had to try and solve the meaning of all the sentences and memorize the total operation described. Even after the teacher's urging to look for such signals, the significance of 'again' was ignored for some time though obvious ones such as 'first' were quickly located.

The discussion showed that none of the group despite previous teaching and observation really knew the significance and function of a valve. Equally they felt that air was not a gas and suggested that it should be expelled along with the waste gases, so revealing that they did not understand the principle of petrol mixing with air to provide the explosive gas. The teacher had previously been confident that the group had a command of all this information and one wonders what further difficulties might have been occasioned if the process had been expressed in the passive mood as would be normal in science texts for the secondary school.

Modelling

In the carrying out of our daily responsibilities as well as in study type learning it is constantly necessary to analyse and organize information. For efficiency in this field of activity help in terms of extracting, organizing, representing and memorizing the material needed can be found in models.

Models include many forms of representational device and are useful in a variety of situations for differing purposes for example:

pictures	to summarize the events of a story or represent an activity or process
maps	to reveal spatial relationships
diagrams	to show processes or describe relationships
flow diagrams	to show orders of events or actions and to separate main and subordinate ideas
graphs	to represent or analyse numerical information
matrices	to analyse information in a form which is easily read and may aid decisions
decision trees	to decide on relevant questions and their order of importance so that a judgement may be made.

Again these devices though most helpful in terms of teaching may be used to observe children's needs. They aid the detection of faulty thinking, inadequately formed concepts and the efficiency of comprehension. Further, they betray any difficulties in the appreciation of relationships, order and ability to work towards a clear purpose.

Example Ten *Smugglers*

Here a ten-year-old boy of average ability was asked to read

Children's Words

a short story based upon the adventures of smugglers in the eighteenth century and then to draw a map to illustrate what happened. This exercise involves the picking out of the main ideas related to the events which were described.

The story

> Out of the darkness came a small boat, dimly lit by a dying moon. Its keel grated on the sand. The waves lapped quietly on the beach. Four men slipped out of the boat and into the water. Each man lifted a keg from the boat and on to his shoulders. They waded ashore, walked over the beach and quietly put the kegs down inside a dark cave, hidden at the foot of the cliffs. Back to the boat they went for more kegs and all the time they kept a sharp look-out for Excise men who might see them from the top of the cliffs.
>
> These men were smugglers. The small boat had come from a large ship anchored some way out at sea. They were smuggling kegs of brandy from France. Soon, on another dark night, the kegs would be taken from the cave to some lonely barn or inn. From there they would be sold secretly, one or two at a time. The brandy could be sold at less than the usual price because the smugglers had avoided the duty, or tax, which should have been paid when the brandy was brought into the country.
>
> This was how smuggling was done in the 18th century. At lonely spots on the coast, brandy, wines, tobacco and many other things, were brought ashore secretly. Sometimes the smugglers were caught by the Excise men. Then they were condemned to hard labour, often abroad.

Commentary

The boy limits his representational map to only the first of

Diagnostic teaching

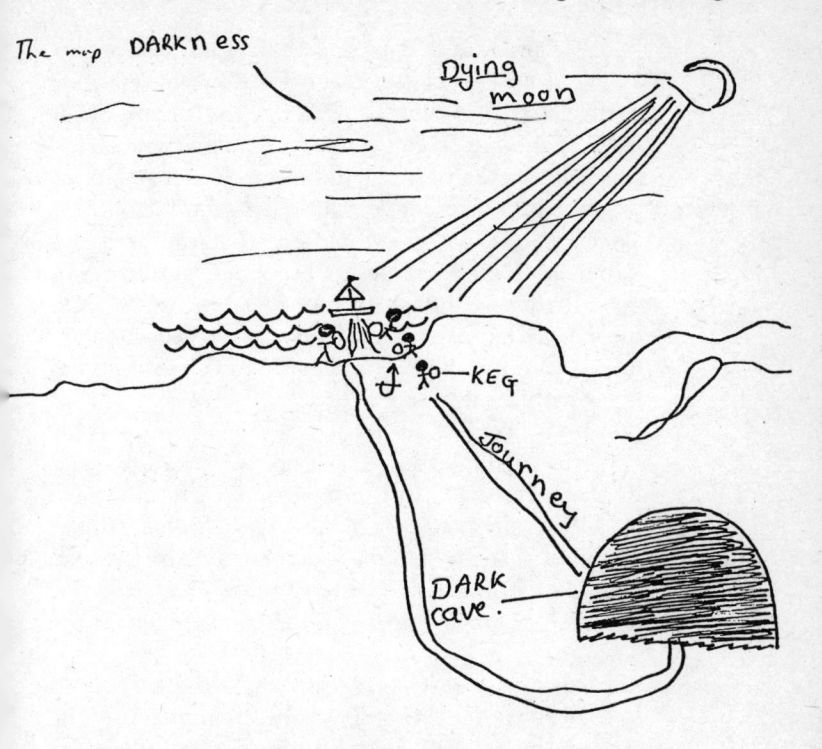

the three paragraphs and the secondary stage of the operation described in the second paragraph is omitted. Admittedly this second part requires rather more imaginative representation than the first or even a second picture, but although the boy was aware that he could create more than one picture to express the story this latter avenue was not employed.

It is also interesting that the child feels it necessary to add labels to his drawing – no doubt from the realization that in terms of both realism and artistic quality his drawing is rather immature.

Most of the elements of the first paragraph are included but there are some errors and omissions as follows:

(a) the dying moon is a new moon. This could be lack of

knowledge for it is hard to believe that the concept 'dying' is not understood. However, some weighting to this latter possibility is given by the strength of the rays emanating from the moon. In discussion afterwards it was clear that he did not realize that a dying moon would give out very little light and he had not associated with it the comment that the area was 'dimly lit'. He said in fact that the men would need a good light to find their way to the cave. We see therefore the influence of poorly formed concepts linked with a lack of appreciation of the cohesion of ideas within the passage.

(b) there is a peculiar addition of a second route to the cave almost suggesting that it has two entrances and the men returned to the boat by a different route than that taken to reach the cave. None of this is included in the text and as such it may have been an imaginative addition. The boy suggested afterwards, however, that this information was included in the passage.

(c) the drawings of the men are so minimal that it would have been rather difficult to show them carrying the kegs on their shoulders or keeping a watchful eye for Excise men. However, on being asked to demonstrate how the smugglers carried the kegs he held out his hands in front of his stomach. He did not know what excise meant but on being given the substitute term customs men he was able to understand that reference in the passage.

Diagnostic teaching

Example Eleven *Irrigation*
(Here an eleven-year-old girl of average ability was asked to draw two pictures to demonstrate the two types of irrigation described in the stimulus passage.)

The account

> The bringing of water to dry land is called irrigation. It has been used for thousands of years in countries where they have very little rain. Although there are many different ways of irrigating there are two *main* methods – flowing and sprinkling. Flowing, or flow irrigation, is used on flat land near a river. A canal is cut from the river. From the main canal, run smaller canals and from these, even smaller canals, called field channels, take the water to the crops.
>
> In hilly country, the water has to be pumped from the river to storage tanks on high ground. From here, it runs down through wide pipes and into narrow pipes which have holes pierced in them. The water squirts up through the holes like fountains and sprinkles the land.
>
> The river Nile flows through Egypt, another dry country. But for the Nile, very few people would be able to live there. In the old days it would overflow its banks in the wet season and almost dry up in the dry season. Sometimes, the wet season failed to come and then there was a drought and famine in the land.
>
> The tribes living in Egypt had to get their water from wells. But very little water could be brought to the land in this way.
>
> In recent years, huge dams have been built on the river. The dams hold back the water in deep lakes. In this way, the water can be stored in the wet season and used in the dry season, the river is controlled so that it no longer overflows and the canals are kept fed.

Children's Words

The map and representation

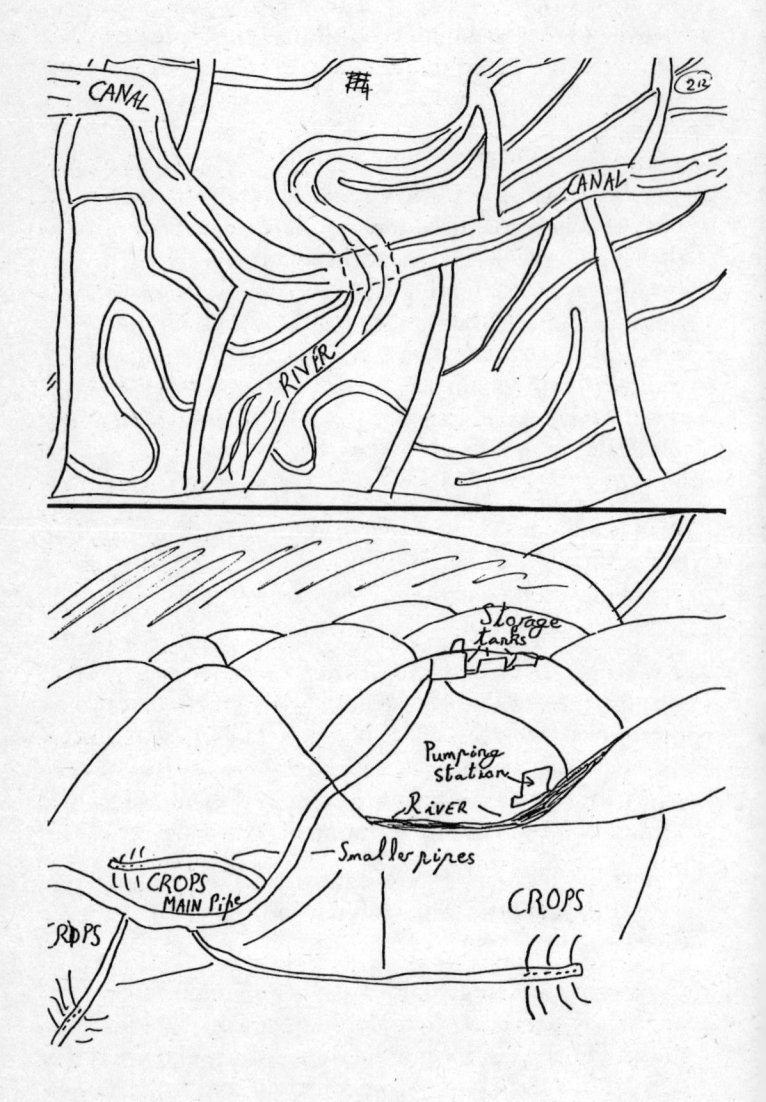

Commentary

The girl makes a reasonable attempt at this representation. However, in the flow irrigation drawing it is interesting that she depicts the canal being cut through the river rather than from it, a detail admittedly but one of some importance. Equally she shows a number of main canals. Whereas this may be a reasonable addition, the fact that one such canal rejoins the river is not acceptable and would be likely to have serious consequences for the irrigation flow.

Her artistic ability seems to have let her down in the representation of the sprinkling method for the river appears to have nowhere to go. The position of the pumps, storage tanks and the dispersion of the pipes is satisfactory but no pipe is shown joining the pumps with the storage tanks. Her explanation of the single line which might appear to represent this was that it was a footpath so that the men could inspect the tanks. This omission is interesting for the need for a pipe from the pumps to the storage tanks is not mentioned as such in the passage. Inference was therefore necessary but this inference was not made until she was asked how she thought the water got from the pumps to the storage tanks. This omission of inferential information is a common problem for children and may here stem from an overemphasis on oral reading and literal interpretation during past instruction or be contributed to by a lack of experience in tasks which demand the relation of knowledge to new material. It can be seen, however, that activities of this type are helpful in focussing the teacher's and child's attention on only those elements which are essential to a complete comprehension of the text.

Example Twelve *Sky diving*
Two ten-year-old boys were asked to draw pictures after reading a passage concerned with parachute jumping. The first a boy some one year behind his chronological age in terms of attainment drew the picture on the spot jumping

section and the other whose attainment was about a year in advance of his age completed the picture representing free fall techniques.

The Account

Many people like to do exciting things – some on land, some on water and some in the air. One of the most exciting things you can do in the air is parachute jumping. Thousands of people have learned this sport, but it takes courage, calm nerves and discipline.

Parachutists often do their first jump from a tower which is about 80 m high.

Competitions are held in different countries by the National Aeronautic Association to see who is World Champion. The first competition was held in 1951 in Yugoslavia and people from five other countries took part.

There are two kinds of competition. The first is called 'spot jumping'. In this, the jumper tries to land as near as he can to a marked spot on the ground. He steers himself towards the spot by pulling the cords of his parachute.

The second kind is called 'free fall' or 'sky diving'. In this, the jumper falls through the air for hundreds of metres before he pulls the rip-cord to open his parachute.

There are strict rules about sky diving. Anyone who breaks the rules is not allowed to jump again. There is no place here for people who just like to show-off. One rule is that you must open your parachute before you get to 670 m above the ground.

Another rule is that every sky diver has to carry two parachutes. If the first one fails to open, he has the second one to rely on. The second parachute is hardly ever needed.

By the time the jumper pulls his rip-cord, he is falling very fast and the opening of the parachute causes a severe shock. This shock has now been lessened by a 'sleeve' in a panel of the parachute, which checks its rate of opening.

When he is falling, and before his parachute has opened, the jumper uses his arms and legs to steer himself. He uses them just as a bird uses its wings and tail when it is gliding. He lands at about 16 km/h and he has to know how to roll over when he hits the ground. If he stayed stiff, he might break his legs.

Parachute jumping is now safer than mountaineering, football, or boxing. In France learners made 100,000 parachute jumps without a single accident. They were safe because they remembered to obey the rules.

Commentary (spot jumping)

This effort shows both a lack of comprehension and a certain naivety of general understanding. For example the aeroplane is in a position before the jump took place rather than after it, the parachute though open is not supporting the man's weight and such activity is unlikely to take place in such a mountainous area. Though the passage is simple and direct the child's illustration demonstrates the crucial importance to comprehension of background knowledge. Frequently we underestimate the contribution to understanding of a text which is made by general knowledge and conceptual development; having such understandings ourselves we tend to be unaware of how much we draw upon them as we read. Thus we are often guilty of overestimating the children's ability on the one hand and underestimating the difficulty of tasks we give them on the other.

This boy missed one essential main idea in the brief passage which was relevant to his task, namely he does not show the jumper steering himself towards the marked spot by pulling on the cords of his parachute. Later discussion drew

Children's Words

Representation (spot jumping)

188

this fact to the boy's attention but the likelihood is that the illustration with all its confusion would have represented those items committed to memory had he not been asked to make the illustrative response and so reveal his misconceptions for correction.

Free fall

This boy makes an interesting attempt, producing three illustrations to depict the chronological order of events. He has obviously gained a good general impression of the main facts but then embroiders them in an imaginative fashion, creating altitudes for various operations mentioned but for which such precise numerical information is not provided. In discussion these extra figures proved to be his own logical analysis of the passage and not the product of previous knowledge. Such behaviour is often provided by children of above average ability but in this case could be a little dangerous if memorized and later acted upon.

A number of important items, however, are omitted – the second parachute, the pulling of the rip cord and the sleeve which checks the rate of opening of the parachute. The boy had interpreted the sleeve as being a slit in the sleeve of the parachutist's clothing rather than being related to the parachute. Thus his literal concept of the word sleeve misled him. Again we can see how the picture demonstration can reveal information about a child's language and thinking which other types of observation may not open up.

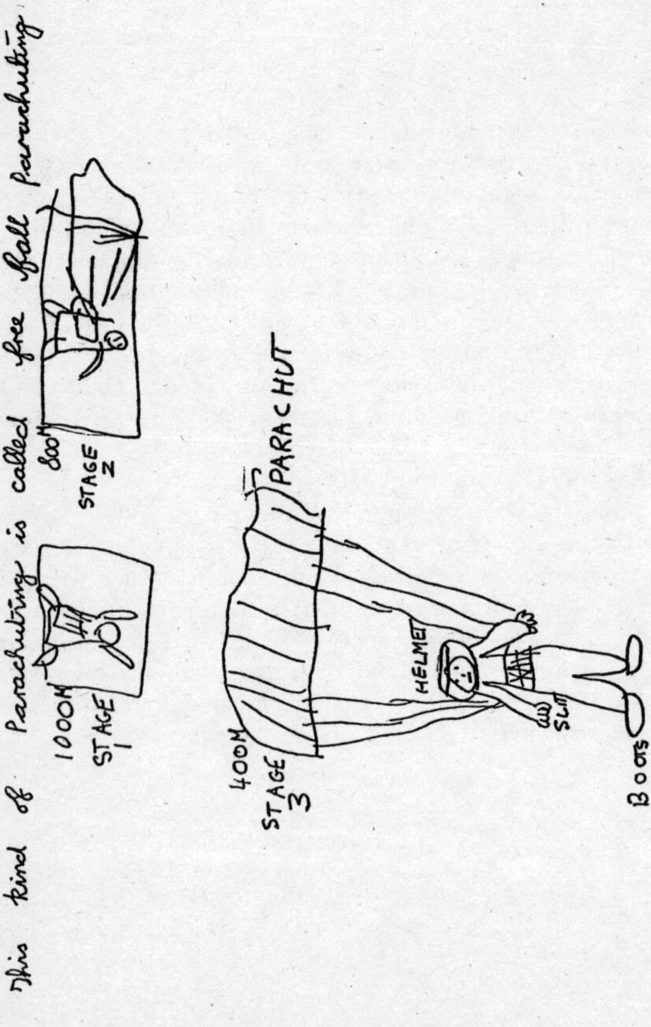
This kind of Parachuting is called free fall Parachuting
1000M
STAGE 1
800M
STAGE 2
400M
STAGE 3
PARACHUT
HELMET
BOOTS

Diagnostic teaching

Example Thirteen *Who likes animals?*
(A nine-year-old girl of above average ability was asked to read the following passage and then represent as briefly as possible an answer to the question 'Why do people kill animals?')

The text

Most people are very kind to animals – but some people who like animals sometimes have to kill them. Some people kill animals because they are pests – rats, rabbits and foxes, for instance. Some people kill animals to provide us with food. And some people hunt animals for sport. Some hunt animals they can eat, some hunt pests, and some just hunt for pleasure.

Representation

```
                    hunt for pests
                          ↑
hunt for food  ←  [ people kill animals ]  →  kills pests
                    ↙              ↘
      because they are ill      hunt for pleasure
```

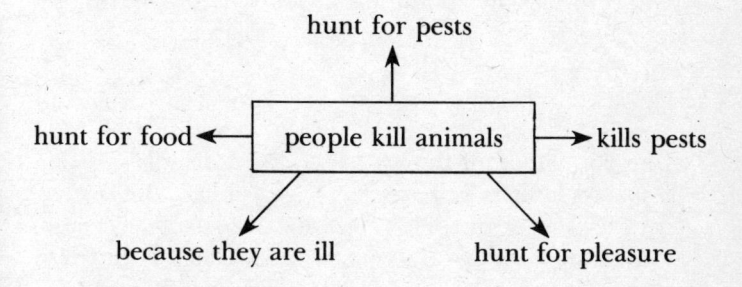

Commentary

The idea of killing because they might be ill is an addition in terms of the passage rather than a misrepresentation of the author's meaning. But the idea of hunting for food is a slight but nevertheless an omission in relation to the passage and the question. The addition shows the power of prior knowledge and thinking but the omission indicates a slight lack of attention to the detail supplied by the author.

Children's Words

Example Fourteen *The World's Population*
A group of fifteen-year-old children of average ability undertaking a topic on World Population found it difficult to envisage the way in which the population of the world had suddenly expanded after reading the following passage. And they found it even more difficult to appreciate that whereas the percentage of illiterate people in the world had consistently fallen this century the actual number of people who were illiterate had in fact risen. A good deal of discussion took place but failed to find a solution to the problem. Eventually the following graph was produced by the group which whilst it answered their original question involved them in a discovery that many of the graphs produced for publicity purposes in brochures and on television deceived them because they did not obey the basic rules of this type of representation media. Which led them quite naturally into a survey of publicity material of this type and the further detection of bias and prejudice in publicity brochures.

The account

> The population of the world has been steadily growing almost as long as we have had records but in the last few decades it has grown at an alarming rate. In 600 AD there were about 500 million people. The population expanded and by the year 1800 AD the whole world still had only 800 million people. Yet by 1900 AD there were over 1,500 million people and in 1980 there were nearly 4,000 million people.
>
> An old Persian legend partially explains how this has happened. A courtier once gave a king a chessboard. The king was so pleased that he asked the courtier what he would like in return. The courtier asked for grains of rice – one for the first square, two for the second square, four for the third, eight for the fourth, thirty-two grains for the sixth square and so. The king's rice barns were empty

Diagnostic teaching

World population and literacy

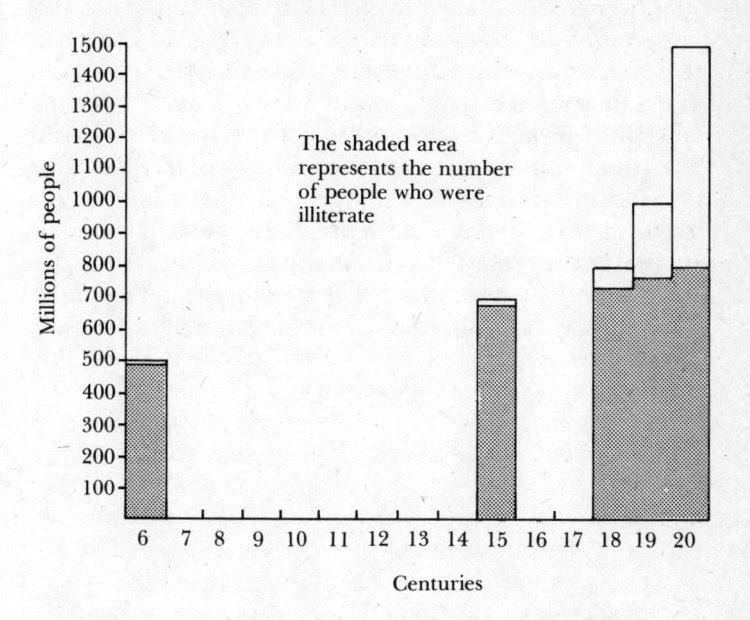

[Bar chart: x-axis "Centuries" from 6 to 20, y-axis "Millions of people" from 100 to 1500. Bars at century 6 (~500), century 15 (~680), century 18 (~800, shaded to ~720), century 19 (~1000, shaded to ~750), century 20 (~1500, shaded to ~800). Note: "The shaded area represents the number of people who were illiterate"]

long before they got to the sixty-fourth square on the board.

In just the same way when the world's population was small it could only grow slowly, but the larger it became the more quickly it could grow.

There are other things which have helped the population to grow. Because of better food supplies, cleanliness and modern medicine fewer babies die and most people live a lot longer. In 1870 225 out of every 1,000 babies born died but by 1970 only 15 out of every 1,000 died before their first birthday. In 1900 the average life expectancy was 47 years but in 1970 it was 75 years.

Now the world's population is so large that the resources and food supplies needed to support us all may soon run out. Already nearly half the world's population do not have enough food to keep them healthy.

Children's Words

Case Study

The validity of diagnostic teaching, as has been insisted throughout, depends upon two basic factors. Firstly the observation of the child's needs must be undertaken in relation to normal activities within the language across the curriculum context. Secondly every effort must be made to overcome subjectivity in the interpretation of the child's responses. In addition the whole process should be one of gradual growth based in a hypothesis-testing approach. To demonstrate the procedure and also to give an example involving work at sixth form level to balance the weighting of the earlier examples towards the primary school this chapter concludes with a summary of a case study.

The background

Jimmy, a boy of almost seventeen years, was a student at an open access sixth form college. He was studying for 'O' levels in mathematics, technical drawing, computer studies and biology and C.S.E. in English language. The staff expressed concern about his progress specifically mentioning his reading ability and spelling. The school had administered the Gapadol Reading test and he attained a score of fourteen years nine months.

Jimmy had undertaken his secondary education in three different schools as a result of family movement. He was seen as something of an isolate within the college though from a work point of view all his attitudes appeared to be positive for he was neat, well organized, punctual and highly cooperative.

The Gapadol is a cloze test and an analysis of Jimmy's errors showed possible difficulty in the closure of verbs, adverbs, prepositions and intersentential conjunctives. These possibilities were further examined by cloze passages from the materials which he was using in school and one example follows which was taken from the book he was reading for personal enjoyment.

Factory of Death

December 1942 was a busy month for the men who administered Auschwitz. In the first place, _____ was coming; and, while the birth of the Infant Jesus was scarcely an event hallowed in _____ gospels, the S.S., nevertheless, like so many who wallow in cruelty, wallowed also in sentimentality. _____ would burn without scruples, indeed with patriotic fervour, one thousand children; but their eyes would grow misty when they swapped pictures of their own loved ones at home.

_____ Christmas could not be ignored, particularly when they were surrounded by a bunch of bloody Jews who did not believe in _____ and whose barbaric forefathers had crucified the Saviour in the first place. The problem was how they could acknowledge _____ event without relaxing what they called euphemistically discipline; and this they solved simply by making it compulsory that in every barracks, prisoners should sing in chorus 'Silent Night'. _____ who sang badly, it was decreed, were sent to bed without supper.

So every evening after work, we men of Canada, stood before Block Senior Polzakiewicz. A _____ borrowed from the orchestra drew gently on his bow and we began to bawl out the words of this fine old _____. For those of us who spoke _____, of course, it was not a particularly onerous duty; but those who did not, most of the Poles, for instance, had a hard time.

Polzakiewicz would tear his hair as they mangled the beautiful old German words. Then _____ would churn among the ranks, trying to beat the _____ into their thick skulls with his club, as a result of which few of them slept, to quote the carol, in heavenly peace.

Table 10 Closures

Passage	Student
Christmas	√
Nazi	the
they	√
therefore	(omitted)
Santa Claus	√
the	√
those	√
violinist	man
carol	song
German	(omitted)
he	√
words	hell

Commentary

It was obvious that Jimmy did not enjoy cloze tasks nor had he, probably through lack of practice, developed any stragegy for attacking the task. However the earlier observations were confirmed. He appeared not to have difficulty with closures involving nouns, pronouns or adjectives but his problems seemed to centre most on items which are important to the cohesion of the passage. It is noteworthy that here the second closure 'nazi' is omitted and discussion afterwards suggested that this could be due either to a limited concept of the word 'gospel' and a lack of awareness of the significance of the lower case 'g' or the use of 'scarcely' as a hidden negative and relational clues offered by 'while' and 'nevertheless'.

To gain further insights, Jimmy read another passage from the *Factory of Death* orally.

Diagnostic teaching

Text and analysis Factory of Death

It was just nine o'clock in the evening of June 30, 1942, a pleasant time for dusk was falling, cloaking the blemishes, mellowing the mundane, accentuating beauty with its gentle half light. I could see shrubs and trees, which made a soothing contrast to the desolation and the awful nothingness which surrounded my last base; and mentally I chalked up a point in favour of Auschwitz.

My shoes, too, were making an unfamiliar sound as I marched. I was on a concrete road again, a civilised road, away from the crumbling dust, the rubble, the decay of Maidanek. Point number two for Auschwitz.

These, of course, were only fleeting first impressions, no more than barely conscious thoughts. My mind was focused mainly on what lay ahead, on the camp which until now had been just a dark, brooding hulk in the dusk and which, as we drew closer, was revealing some of its details.

I had seen the searchlight as soon as I had dropped from the wagon. Static, unwinking, it played on the entrance, spilling out about fifty yards around it. Now we were within its pale, in sight of the tall double gates with their fine wire mesh; of the watch tower, cradle of the searchlight; of the S.S.

It was these men in their faultless green uniforms who gave me my first inkling that Auschwitz was different from any other place I had ever known. I had seen many S.S. men before, but none quite like these. They were lined up on the right-hand side of the road a few yards apart, statuesque figures, holding the leashes of alsatian dogs in their left hands, sub-machine guns in their right. Their faces were impassive. Their still, erect figures exuded an air of cold, bloodless efficiency; and the sight of them puzzled me.

Children's Words

Table 11 Analysis

Text word	Miscue	Meaning	Syntax	Grapho-phonic similarity
Mundane	moonl			✓
accentuating	accompanying		✓	✓
desolation	desolate	✓		✓
crumbling	clouding	✓	✓	✓
These	Those	✓	✓	✓
lay	lie	✓	✓	✓
drew	draw	✓	✓	✓
had seen	saw	✓		
static	status			✓
fifty	thirty	✓	✓	✓
searchlight	sunlight		✓	✓
the	their			✓
leashes	lashes		✓	✓
impassive	impressive		✓	✓
efficiency	efficient	✓		✓

Commentary

It became evident during the reading that Jimmy had a slight articulation difficulty which it was discovered related back to a partially overcome speech defect in earlier years. Clearly the speech problem was at least partially responsible for his retiring disposition and his fear of performing before his peers and isolation from them.

The miscue analysis shows a strong grapho-phonic similarity between the stimulus word and the miscue. However, it will be noted that the departures are all in the middle or at the ends of words suggesting that Jimmy may superimpose his own expectations upon the text rather too heavily. The number of miscues from this one passage are really insufficient for a thorough-going analysis but the general trend of behaviour was confirmed by the use of other passages, and by comparing the miscues made to his answers to questions based upon them. The answers are heavily based in background knowledge and often have only a tenuous relationship to the passage. He seems to try to impose his own knowledge upon the text rather than accommodate his knowledge and expectancy with the structure and meaning of the text.

Observation of Jimmy's normal classwork suggested that although he was slow, he was quite capable of extracting isolated facts from a text but he equally reveals an inability to vary his reading style to take account of his own specific purposes for reading or differing types of reading media. For example he proved incapable of skimming for he could not ignore information which was irrelevant to his needs. Equally he always read in a linear fashion which makes heavy demands upon the memory. He had difficulty in recognizing the framework of a text and seemed only to synthesize meaning at the phrase and sentence level whereas the efficient reader creates a structure based upon the interrelationship of the ideas and information. Thus given a sequencing task he performed well but when asked to precis a section from the text used in biology, his favourite subject, he could not separate the main from the subordinate ideas.

Text and analysis: modelling activity

To further examine these difficulties Jimmy was given a modelling task from some material he was currently using. Giving as it does an extra element in the form of the visual channel, modelling gives a further opportunity to recognize and express the meaning relationships present in the text.

The acquisition of new knowledge about a problem does not always help scientists solve it. Sometimes it complicates the original problem. A striking example of this occurred when the findings of the International Indian Ocean Expedition were reported in 1962.

Oceanographers have long been perplexed by the fact that there is so little sediment on the floors of the world's oceans. Their calculations, based on the estimated rate of sediment accumulation and on the time this process has had to work, indicate that there should be a layer of sand, rock particles, and organic matter from two to two and one-half miles thick over the bottom of the seas. Their findings of the actual thickness of the sediment layer, however, have indicated that it is not more than a fourth of this depth. (Some oceanographers believe the deposit of organic material alone, falling in what they call the 'rain of death', would have accounted for this amount of sediment.)

Then in 1962 the expedition scientists reported that they found the bottom of the Indian Ocean much rougher than had been thought. To the oceanographers, this means that their estimates of the actual thickness of the sediment layer have been too high.

Thus it may be that an even thinner layer of sediment exists than that which oceanographers had previously considered too small.

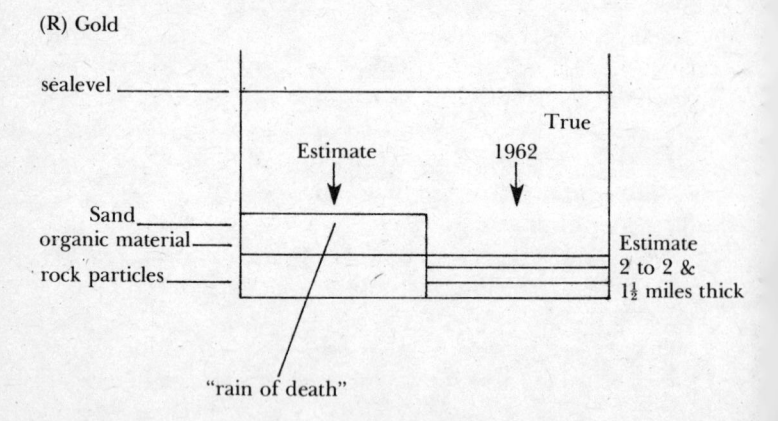

(R) Gold

sealevel ─────────

Estimate ↓   True 1962 ↓

Sand ─────
organic material ─────
rock particles ─────

Estimate 2 to 2 & 1½ miles thick

"rain of death"

Diagnostic teaching

Commentary

Jimmy's model suggests that he understood the general point regarding the sediment but he wrongly suggests that the sand, rock particles and organic matter were in separate layers. His response concerning the depth of the layers of sediment shows an over-ready acceptance of the reduced estimate and an ignoring of the information concerning the roughness of the sea bed. He also ignores the question marks which the author suggests still remain.

It is interesting that none of the words used on the model indicate a relationship yet the author quite clearly sets out such in his description and the form of meaning is reinforced by the style and the vocabulary.

First hypothesis 'Calculations . . . indicate'
Observation 'however'
New hypothesis 'indicated'
New observation 'Then'
New hypothesis 'Thus'

Jimmy did not perceive the semantic relationships or their linguistic markers. In all his work he is a passive recipient never an active processor of language and meaning. Language processing and study techniques are both at a rather lowly level for his age and the type of work he is undertaking and he has the further blockage from his rather retiring nature. The best hope of revitalizing his language usage and thinking will be through extensive discussion with him of his reading strategies and the comprehension of his texts based upon modelling and precis-type tasks.

4

Language across the curriculum

The aim of undertaking the development of children's thinking and the language arts in the holistic and realistic setting of the total curriculum is by no means easy to realize. The major difficulties would appear to be

(a) ensuring that all aspects of language are given appropriate amounts of attention so that there is a balanced appreciation and usage of each type. It would be easy, for example in working heavily through the medium of topic work, to omit opportunities for contact with imaginative literature.

(b) integrating the mastery of language strategies, techniques and skills rather than hoping for development through separate skill-getting activities.

(c) achieving the effective organization of teaching and learning situations. This is especially difficult in the subject specialism-type timetabling of work within the majority of our secondary schools for here all teachers must be involved in the development of language as each subject area makes its own peculiar demands. The problem is not simply that of the English teacher but equally there must be some coordination or the children could be placed in a situation

Language across the curriculum

where there is excessive repetition and overlap in the language learning to which they are exposed.

It is crucially important therefore that all schools adopt an agreed language policy, support this with planning, organization and recording systems and also review all aspects of the work at regular intervals.

In chapter 2 we looked at general teaching strategies for holistic learning and in chapter 3 at the objectives for language learning and diagnostic teaching devices for the development and observation of the strategies of language usage. It finally remains important to set out the major questions to be asked in the formulation of a language policy and suggest mechanisms which may be helpful in planning and recording the day-to-day work within the classroom.

Major questions for the formulation of a language policy

1 What is to be the philosophical position concerning the role of the teacher and the expected behaviour of the children?

2 How is the teaching to be organized — on a class teaching, team teaching or subject specialist basis?

3 How, if at all, is the teaching to be timetabled?

4 Is there to be any grouping or streaming of the children?

5 What role is to be given to the physical and social environment? (e.g. the contribution by the parents and the use to be made of the environment as a stimulus for or the content of learning).

6 How are the material resources of the school to be organized?

7 What proposals are there for the expansion, retention, classification and use of child produced resources?

8 What proposals are to be made concerning the enrichment of the language experiences of the children?

9 How is general cognitive development to be stimulated through language work?

10 What balance of time among the language arts is appropriate for the various age and ability groups?

11 How can it be ensured that strategies and skills appropriate to each stage are developed?

12 How can it be ensured that the child is involved in making use of all the language functions and developing the thinking appropriate to the wide range of language tasks and media?

13 What provisions are to be made for planning at school, class and individual levels and what type of recording system is to be introduced.

14 Are any special arrangements to be made for children who experience difficulties?

All these questions lead to many others which are of a more detailed nature. Inevitably as the subdivisions are explored the considerations become more specialized in terms of the particular institution, its staff and children. The problem which so often arises is that in producing the details of a language policy, the details of the skills take over and the holistic and realistic nature of the intended approach to language development is lost as activities begin to be devised to impart particular skills rather than to ensure their use. Nevertheless, without some such questioning and planning the work is likely to become directionless despite the integrated learning approach.

Planning and matrices

(a) It is useful to list all the major activities which are to be or have been undertaken by the children and form them into matrices to check the range and balance of coverage given to other important aspects of development. Some of these have already been listed and discussed in detail and so will not be repeated here – such as the objectives for the language across the curriculum approach, the skills to be developed, and the functions of various types of language usage.

(b) In addition it is important that each child is given experiences which develop the full range of human roles. In major heading form these are five-fold:
>   home and family
>   employment
>   leisure
>   consumer
>   community life

(c) As the various forms of written language media have different styles and purposes, and demand rather different attack from the reader, it is important to see that the children are exposed to the widest possible range. The following list may act as a guide:

Fiction   Textbooks   Reference books   Journals
Magazines   Newspapers   Comics   Brochures
Fliers   Advertisements and notices   Legal
documents   Reports and Minutes   Forms and
Questionnaires   Regulations   Instructions
Letters   Signs and Symbols

A final word

Whatever the teaching ideas, planning and recording devices, the reader should by now be in no doubt that this approach makes immense demands upon both teacher and parent. *Firstly* it is their role to ensure the stimulation of needs and interests to challenge the child, to expand his horizons and linguistic abilities and at the same time retain a balance among all aspects of language. *Secondly* they must be constantly vigilant in observing the child's needs and any signs of an imbalance in development or the seeds of possible learning difficulties. *Thirdly* they must be ready and able to give support and teaching to develop skills and strategies at any moment that the child has a need of such help.

All this adds up to a considerable drain upon the creativity, imagination, understanding and organizational powers. But then success in language learning is far more dependent upon the interested adults in a child's life than any other agency or materials. The adults' enthusiasm, understanding and energy are more important than all other factors.

References

Ausubel, D.P. (1968) *Educational Psychology: a cognitive perspective*. New York: Holt, Rinehart & Winston.

Bruner, J.S. (1974) *Beyond the Information Given*. London: Allen & Unwin.

(Bullock Committee) Department of Education and Science (1975) *A Language for Life*. London: HMSO.

Flesch, R. (1955) *Why Johnny Can't Read*. New York: Harper & Row.

Lunzer, E. and Gardner, W.K. (1979) *The Effective Use of Reading*. London: Heinemann Educational Books.

Merritt, J.E. (1971) *Reading and the Curriculum*. London: Ward Lock Educational.

Merritt, J.E. et al. (1972) *Correspondence Texts of the Reading Development Course — E.261*. Milton Keynes: Open University.

Merritt, J.E. (1975) *What Shall We Teach?* London: Ward Lock Educational.

Morris, J.M. (1975) In D. Moyle (ed.) *Reading: What of the Future?* London: Ward Lock Educational.

Moyle, D. (1979) 'Informal testing of reading needs', in Raggett, M. St. J. et al., *Assessment and Testing or Reading*. London: Ward Lock Educational.

Moyle, D. (ed) (1981) *Language Patterns*. Eastbourne: Holt, Rinehart & Winston.

Murphy, R. (1973) *Adult Functional Literacy*. Educational Testing Services.

Parker, D.H. (1958) *Schooling for Individual Excellence*. London: Thomas Nelson.
Southgate, V., Arnold, H. and Johnson, S. (1981) *Extending Beginning Reading*. London: Heinemann.

Suggestions for further reading

Moyle, D. (1978) *Teaching Reading Seminar*. London: Holmes McDougall.
  A set of readings, study suggestions and activities which provides a resource to develop the understandings, teaching and diagnostic techniques outlined in this volume.

Gurney, R. (1976) *Language, Learning and Remedial Teaching*. London: Edward Arnold.
  Presents and discusses in detail the arguments for a reappraisal of attitudes to and teaching approaches for children with language difficulties.

Gatherer, W. A. and Jeffs, R. B. (1980) *Language Skills through the Secondary Curriculum*. London: Holmes McDougall.
  A symposium with study questions which introduce the reader to the full range of knowledge positions and controversies which should be considered in relation to developing the use of language across the curriculum in the secondary school.

Halliday, M.A.K. (1975) *Learning How to Mean*. London: Edward Arnold.
  The first real attempt to classify language development in terms of the functions for which language is used.

Britton, J. (1970) *Language and Learning*. Harmondsworth: Penguin.

> A text which argues for an integrated approach to the learning and teaching of language

Bruner, J. (1974) *The Process of Education*.

> A text which heavily challenges traditional views of learning and techniques of teaching and suggests a new framework for the design of learning situations.

Smith, F. (1975) *Comprehension and Learning*. New York: Holt, Rinehart & Winston.

> A detailed exposition of the psycholinguistic view of language learning and processing.

Tiedt, S.W. and I.M. (1978) *Language Arts Activities for the Classroom*. Allyn & Bacon.

> A most useful volume of suggestions for activities to develop the full range of language abilities.

Moyle, D. (1976) *The Teaching of Reading*. London: Ward Lock Educational (4th Edition).

> A general manual on the teaching of reading.

Torbe, M.M. (1977) *Teaching Spelling*. London: Ward Lock Educational.

> Discusses research into the learning and teaching of spelling and describes teaching strategies.

Donaldson, M. (1978) *Children's Minds*. London: Fontana.

> This book brings new light to the study of children's thinking and gives examples of how the higher thought processes can be developed and used at earlier ages than had previously been thought to be the case.

Sykes, E. and Moyle, D. (1982) *Reading Games and Activities*. New York: Holt, Rinehart & Winston.

> A manual of activities to provide for the consolidation of learning in the early stages of reading development among slow learning children.

Index

adult literacy, 6–8, 15, 31, 207
attitudes, 15–16, 18, 19, 30–32, 92–3, 152, 161
auditory perception, 11–12, 69–71

Breakthrough to Literacy, 41
Bruner, J.S., 11, 37
Bullock Report, 6, 8, 207

case study, 194–201
cloze procedure, 54, 161–7, 175, 177, 194
   nature of, 161
   preparation of, 161–3
   examples of, 164–7, 195–6
   discussions, 162, 166–7
comparative reading, 54–5, 83–6
comprehension, 14–16, 76, 93–4, 143, 146–50, 151, 160, 168–9, 175–193
context cues, 16–17, 54, 93, 153, 161–7
cooperative reading, 53–4, 71–3, 83–6, 169–78

diagnosis,
   hypothesis testing model, 27–8, 66–8, 88–201
   medical model, 25–7, 64–5
diagnostic teaching, 27–8, 33, 64–8, 88–201
   problems of, 89–90

discussion, 51–5, 71–3, 75–6, 78, 81–3
   relationship to language-experience and story method, 51–2
   informal and structured, 51–5, 71–3, 96
   structured examples, 97–141
   diagnosis from, 97–141

English as a second language, 18, 148–9

Flesch, R., 35, 207
frustration level, 151, 154

grammar, 9, 12, 13, 16–17, 52, 64, 72, 92, 95, 101–2, 103, 121, 141, 143, 148, 149, 161, 196

Halliday, M.A.K., 98–100, 207
higher order skills, 14, 83–6, 93–4, 168, 179–93, 199–201

independent level, 151
informal reading inventories, 151–93
instructional level, 151, 154, 159
integrated teaching approach, 56–7
   reservations to, 57–64
   and remedial work, 64–8

211

examples of, 68–87
intermediate skills, 14, 54, 161–7, 168, 176–7
intonation, 9, 101

language across the curriculum, 15, 32, 34, 40–41, 55–7, 202–6
  and remedial work, 64–8
  examples of, 68–87
language curriculum, 91–4
language deficit, 19–21
language development, 9, 17–22, 29–33, 97–141
language difference, 19–21
language difficulty, 15–22, 148–9, 160, 198
language-experience, 21–2, 41–6, 53–4, 57
  advantages, 42–3
  disadvantages, 43–4, 46
  and remedial work, 67
  two types of, 44–6
  examples of, 71–87
language learning, 4, 8–28, 29–33, 55–7, 66–8, 101–2
Language Patterns, 69–77, 81–3, 142, 144, 207
linguistics and reading, 12–13
listening, 9, 75–6, 77
Lunzer, E. & Gardner, W.K., 8, 207

meaning, 9, 11, 13–17
Merritt, J.E., 37, 44, 67, 207
metalinguistic understanding, 6, 31–2
modelling, 79, 85–7, 179–93, 199–200
Morris, J.M., 38–9, 207
Murphy, R., 8, 207

objectives, 5, 91–4
oral reading miscue analysis, 152–61
  limitations of, 152–3
  application of, 154–5
  examples of, 155–61, 197–9

Parker, D.H., 36–7, 207
phonics, 10–12, 16–17, 40–41, 60, 93, 161
  and spelling, 61–2
primary reading skills, 14
programmed learning, 35–7
projects, 74, 78–87
psycholinguistics and reading, 13–16
purpose, 5, 9, 15, 22, 30–32, 37–9, 152

reading media, 15, 32, 82–6, 204–5
reading models, 10–16
reading readiness, 69–81
  tests of, 69–71
reading schemes, 33, 38–9
  and integrated teaching, 55–7, 68–83
reading standards, 1–8
reading-thinking activities, 54, 146, 168–78
  advantages of, 168
  preparation of, 169–70
  prediction, 48–9, 52–4, 71–2, 168–77
  sequencing, 177–8
real life activities, 8, 36–9, 83
remedial education, 21–8, 85–7
retardation, 18, 22–3

skill-getting, 15, 24–5, 34, 36–7
skill learning, 11–12, 24–5
skill-using, 15, 34, 36–7
spelling, 30, 57–8, 61–4
  and reading, 61–2
  teaching method, 61–4
spoken language, 12, 18, 30, 41, 46, 50–51, 91–2
  analysis of, 95–141
  activities, 32, 71–87, 95–141

Index

integration with written language, 41–57, 71–3
story method, 46–51, 53–4, 57
 teaching strategies, 47–9
 advantages of, 50–51
 relationships with language-experience, 46–7, 51
 and remedial work, 67
 examples of, 71–87, 142–50
story retelling, 142–50

teaching methods, 10–16, 34–87
Tough, J., 98–9, 123
transfer of learning, 8, 11–12, 24–5, 36–9

visual perception, 11–12, 18, 69–71
vocabulary, 9, 12, 13, 52, 69–71, 91, 95, 103, 121, 141, 143, 148–9, 181–2, 189

whole word methods, 40–1, 60
word attack skills, 10–13, 16–17, 32, 40, 156
word banks, 63–4, 80
word identification, 10–13, 16–17, 32, 40, 80, 93, 151
writing, 13, 18, 57–61, 73, 82, 84–5, 94–5
written language, 18–19, 41, 52, 87, 92–5